Antimemetics
Why Some Ideas Resist Spreading

Nadia Asparouhova

Antimemetics – Why Some Ideas Resist Spreading

Table of Contents

Escaping Containment	5
Hidden City	27
Drag Coefficient	53
Memetic Galapagos	73
We Are Our Attention	99
Sacred Knowledge	119
Towards Not-Forgetting	139
Acknowledgements	161
Notes	162
Colophon	168

ESCAPING CONTAINMENT

0

HERE'S SOMETHING I'VE NEVER confessed out loud before: I have basically no memory of my life. Every important event, every person who's shaped who I am, every significant conversation I've had – all have slipped through my mind like a sigh and a shadow.

I didn't realize just how poor my episodic memory was until shortly before I began writing this book. It was while browsing the archives of science magazine *Nautilus* that a headline caught my eye: "People Who Can't Picture Sound in Their Minds."[1]

"Huh," I thought. "What does it even mean to picture sound in one's mind?" Skimming through the article, I discovered that someone had given a name to the inability to imagine sounds: *anauralia*.

I had already discovered a few years earlier – thanks to a friend's off-hand comment – that I had *aphantasia*, or the inability to visualize things in one's mind. (Aphantasia is a relatively new concept; it was formally named by a team of researchers at University of Exeter in 2015.) And as a teenager, I had long figured out that I had *synesthesia*: a general term for the crossing of sensory inputs, so that one might taste anger, hear colors, or assign textures, colors, and even personalities to numbers (5, for example, is green to me). Synesthesia helped explain why I felt like such a weirdo during word association icebreaker games ("When I say 'goldfish,' you say…" "…a vast, yawning expanse of glowing light, zooming out rapidly until it shrinks into a tiny dot?"), but otherwise didn't affect my life. Mostly, I found these differences amusing, not distressing. With enough probing, it seemed, everyone's brain was a little bit strange.

So at this point, I wasn't surprised to learn that I didn't hear sounds, either. Truthfully, I had grown a bit weary of reflecting on weird brain phenomena. But further down in the article, I noticed something else:

---

1. Ajdina Halilovic, "People Who Can't Picture Sound in Their Minds," *Nautilus*, February 20, 2024, https://nautil.us/people-who-cant-picture-sound-in-their-minds-517529/.

> *Aphantasia had already been linked with another newly identified but rare syndrome known as Severely Deficient Autobiographical Memory, or SDAM for short. People with SDAM can't relive past experiences in their minds, and a preliminary survey shows just over half of a sample of 2,000 SDAM individuals also have aphantasia.*

"Past experiences?" Now I was confused. Since I was young, I'd maintained a meticulous record of the events of my life, both big and small. I kept a daily log of my work activities. I took notes at every meeting and filed them away, so I could reference what happened in the future.

In recent years, I've let my journaling habit lapse. It takes hours to recount the details of one's life, and at some point I decided I would rather just *live*, instead of trying to record everything that had happened. I thought that my desire to remember things by writing them down was just me being neurotic, while others blissfully let their memories go. But I understood that my decision to let go came with a tradeoff, which was that I would now remember much less of my life than before. Because writing things down is the only way that people can remember their lives. Right? ... Right?

I'm not sure just how "severely deficient" my autobiographical memory is. I am certainly able to recount a stash of key moments in my life and tell stories about them. But upon further reflection, I realized that I "remembered" those stories because I had written detailed accounts of these experiences, then revisited those accounts until they transferred into my long-term memory. I couldn't think of any experience I'd had that I just...remembered, without either a written record, photos, or someone else repeating the story to reinforce the details over time, until they became indistinguishable from fact. I have no memory of any movie, television show, or book I've ever watched or read (or, to be honest: that I've written), though I can usually tell you if I liked them or not. Recalling my memories feels like reciting a poem, or listing all the states in the United States of America, rather than the emotional or visual conjuring up of a moment that other people seem to have. Left to my own devices, I have only very faint scraps and snippets – standing on a beach; sitting in a classroom; a single phrase, fact, or insight from a conversation that I'd memorized – with little to no narrative attached.

I've come to understand my mind as, effectively, a sensory blank canvas, on which every idea is sketched anew. While there is a freedom that comes with this lack of attachment, I do sometimes wonder what I am missing by not remembering the things that others do; whether there are important memories, ideas, connections that I *should* be forming that otherwise escape my mind if I don't write them down.

This realization – that having an exceptionally poor episodic memory was not the default human experience – was more startling than any of the other brain phenomena I'd learned about before. I'd made my way well into adulthood assuming we all worked one way, when it turned out I was the odd one out. Here is the lesson I've learned, over and over again: no matter how confident we are in our version of reality, we don't know what we're missing until someone else points it out.

THIS IS A BOOK about antimemetics: ideas that resist being remembered, comprehended, or engaged with, despite their significance.

Your brain is not so different from mine. We are *all*, in our own ways, entangled in an individual and collective forgetting. For example:

Why do we still observe daylight saving time in the United States, even though a majority of Americans want to get rid of it, and the Senate unanimously passed legislation to abolish it in 2022 – only for such legislation to linger, and ultimately expire, while waiting to be passed by the House of Representatives? If there is little opposition to getting rid of daylight saving time, why does it persist?

Why did it suddenly become acceptable to publicly support nuclear energy after decades of condemnation? In the late 1960s and early 1970s, fear of reactor accidents and nuclear weapons, compounded by bad press from incidents like Three Mile Island and Chernobyl, kept nuclear energy out of clean energy discussions. For thirty-four years, the U.S. Nuclear Regulatory Commission did not approve any licenses to build nuclear reactors. But then something shifted. Film director Oliver Stone produced a documentary, *Nuclear Now*, to argue for its merits; Bill Gates invested $1 billion into building a new nuclear power plant in Wyoming. If nuclear energy was actually a good idea all along, why did it take so long for us to revisit its potential, and how did public sentiment flip so quickly?

Why is handwashing compliance so low, even though we have centuries of evidence demonstrating its effectiveness in preventing the spread of disease? Despite public health campaigns and strong social norms around its importance – no one would admit in polite company that they don't wash their hands – handwashing compliance remains absurdly low. Even among healthcare workers in high-income countries, handwashing rates often hover around 50%.[2] If handwashing is a critical, simple intervention that keeps us safe and healthy, why don't more people do it?

We agree these ideas are important. We are largely aligned on what to do about them. And yet…somehow… when the time comes to doing something about them…the ideas…just…can't…quite…seem…to stay put.

That we can't seem to retain, nor take action on, important ideas might seem like a depressing way of

---

2. JoDee Armstrong-Novak et al., "Healthcare Personnel Hand Hygiene Compliance: Are We There Yet?," *Current Infectious Disease Reports* vol. 25 (2023): 123-129, https://doi.org/10.1007/s11908-023-00806-8.

viewing the world: what's the point of doing anything, then? But instead of resigning ourselves to inaction, I want to ask how we might work *with* these constraints to make progress on important social issues regardless. And that requires taking a deeper look at the shape and characteristics of these ideas.

Our inability to make progress on consequential topics can be at least partly explained by the underlying *antimemetic* qualities that they share – meaning that it is strangely difficult to keep the idea top of mind. My first introduction to antimemetics came in the fall of 2021, when a former colleague and I were trading emails about what he called "memetic engineering research." He was interested in understanding how ideas made their way into public discourse, and whether it was possible to "deterministically shift the Overton window," as he called it, for important ideas.

We, like so many others, had both noticed the discourse was moving from public platforms to private and semi-private ones. The frogs had started to boil in the second half of the 2010s, as people seemed to get angrier, and with much greater intensity, at...just about everything. What first felt like real crises began to feel like being trapped in an episode of the sci-fi show *Lost*, where pushing the button to avert widespread catastrophe became a familiar routine. We were stuck in emergency mode; avoiding disaster had become the central focus of life.

As we approached the end of the decade, the gruesome parts of humanity tumbled into the hot glow of a spotlight. It is uncomfortable to recount these events in writing, even in brief and neutral terms. Just as in war, once the smoke of the battlefield has cleared, it seems transgressive to willingly return to the scene of such violent delights. And yet, in the spirit of resisting antimemesis, I think it is also important to not gloss over the chaos of this as-yet unnamed period of history. So, let me take a deep breath and burble it out to you, which I'll keep to just one paragraph:

Actress Alyssa Milano urged women to share stories of sexual mistreatment under the hashtag #MeToo. White nationalists marched with tiki torches in Charlottesville, Virginia to "Unite the Right." Susan Fowler recounted her experiences with sexual harassment at Uber, triggering a #DeleteUber campaign, an extensive investigation, and CEO Travis Kalanick's eventual ousting. Google employee James Damore published an internal memo complaining about its stifling political culture and questioned the utility of its diversity policies, for which he was fired. Citizens of the United Kingdom voted to break from the European Union, spurred by a new wave of populism. Angry mobbers, equipped with phones, chased down so-called Karens, recording and posting their terror on the internet for all to see. Protests erupted in the first summer of pandemic lockdowns following the murder of George Floyd, along with feverish demands that companies swear public allegiance to the cause or else risk cancellation.

While some decried this era as "cancel culture," others saw it as a reckoning with power dynamics and accountability in a new online social age. As for me, I found myself standing in the living room of my apartment in June of 2020, overlooking the streets of San Francisco with a deep thudding in my stomach, and wondering if the rioters would make it to our neighborhood. Stuck at home under the shelter-in-place order, I suddenly felt vulnerable and afraid. I know now that I was not the only one who felt this way, but at the time, it wasn't okay to voice these fears out loud. Even expressing concerns about my own safety could be perceived as a lack of support for the public cause.

Once, at my old job – several years before the George Floyd riots – security had notified everyone in the all-hands Slack channel to stay inside: there was an active shooter roaming the area outside our office in SoMa, near the ballpark. It was the second shooter in our neighborhood that week.

"Wow, what's up with our neighborhood lately?" I typed into Slack with a bit of anxious humor, hoping that my colleagues would help soothe my nerves. Almost immediately, I received a response from a member of the social impact team. "A lack of access to resources...difficult circumstances...more hardships than any of us will ever understand," came the smooth reply. "I wish them all the best." Just as quickly, her reply was adorned with flashing, blinking emoji reacts from our colleagues, who supported her statement. My face grew hot as I hastily typed out an apology; I didn't know it was a faux pas to express fear of active shooters at the workplace, instead of empathy for those who might be trying to kill me.

The exchange left me rattled. It wasn't just that I had misread the room – it was a sudden awareness that certain thoughts and feelings were now considered out of bounds to share in public settings. From then on, I kept my mouth shut, quietly reserving my concerns for more private, trusted conversations.

People didn't stop feeling scared or isolated or disapproving of what quickly became a cultural narrative spun out of control: they just burrowed further underground. Their hasty retreat fueled the rise of group messaging apps like iMessage, Whatsapp, Telegram, Messenger, and Signal. These applications launched in the late 2000s and early 2010s, but their adoption didn't spread with the same sort of virality that social apps like Facebook, Instagram, or Twitter once did. There was no innate trendiness to these products – no social clout (at first, anyway) to be gained. Group chats were just a utility that people used to talk to their friends.

Unlike most new social apps, getting in on group chats was more like value investing than meme stocks. While COVID did, briefly, spike people's interest in group chats, for the most part, there was no real takeoff moment or hockey stick graph. Adoption simply climbed, slowly and steadily, from a murmur to a clamor.

Only against the backdrop of an increasingly chaotic environment – the public web – did group chats finally take on special meaning as safe spaces and cherished home bases. They were a small, scrappy patch of the online universe where people felt like they could still be themselves. Group chats' true social utility emerged from how they were used, rather than something they set out to be.

Group chats formed the next era of the internet: a dark network of scattered outposts, where no one wants to be seen or heard or noticed, so that they might be able to talk to their friends in peace. All the spiciest takes – not the smooth, polished, hot takes that are distributed performatively for social clout, but the messy, half-formed, honest takes – gravitated from public channels to private group chats. But somehow, ideas continue to spread throughout these seemingly disconnected villages. How do people discover and share these ideas without relying on public modes of transportation?

In the Web 2.0 era – the decade that roughly spans the early 2000s, starting with platforms like Friendster, Myspace, and Facebook, through the mid-2010s, when social media use began to exhume our darker habits and motivations – it was believed that an idea's virality was a hallmark of its value, because it signaled interest and engagement from a wider audience. To be clear, virality was also a hallmark of crap: mounds and mounds of drivel and slop being shoveled and processed and recycled by content farms and middling influencers. But the most valuable ideas *did* seem to wend their way out of the dirt, however slowly, propelled by their ability to captivate people's attention. Not all viral ideas were good, but all good ideas seemed to go viral eventually.

Now, though, the most important ideas seemed to be tunneling *downwards*, deeper into the Earth's crust, like a rare and precious diamond, where no one could find them

– and this was by intention. How was it possible that the most bespoke ideas had become *resistant* to memetic spread? And how did they still manage to spread between groups, while also avoiding public channels?

LIKE NEWTON OBSERVING THE apple falling from a tree before he called it *gravity*, or Darwin observing in the Galapagos how different species adapted to their environments before he called it *evolution*, both I and my ex-colleague (and many others at the time – I certainly don't mean that we were the Newtons or the Darwins in this case!) had noticed that a certain class of ideas had become resistant to viral spread, before we knew to call it *antimemetics*. But a group of people on the internet had noticed this concept long before we had, which they developed in an internet forum for a fictional universe called the SCP Foundation.

The SCP Foundation began as a collaborative online fiction writing community, where dangerous, paranormal creatures are imagined and logged in the style of a bureaucratic investigative agency. ("SCP" stands for "Special Containment Procedures.") The first entry, SCP-173, published in June 2007, describes an entity that is "to be kept in a locked container at all times....if given the chance it will kill anyone within it's line of site [sic]. It's [sic] weakness however is that it does not move while being watched."[3] SCP expanded into a wiki of similarly-themed entries that share a creepy, unsettling style resembling Lovecraftian horror: stoking our fear of the unknown and incomprehensible.

In the early days of the SCP universe, a member of the community named qntm (also known as Sam Hughes, a British writer and software engineer) published an entry for SCP-055, which he described as a "'self-keeping secret' or 'antimeme.'" All information about SCP-055, including its

---

3. S. S. Walrus, "From the Files of Site 19.," archived on archive.is, accessed December 20, 2024, https://archive.is/QD9UF.

origins and characteristics, are unknown, not because they are unknowable, but because they are "self-classifying." The entry, which isn't very long, is worth reading in its entirety, but I can't resist sharing a few of my favorite excerpts:[4]

> *It is not indescribable, or invisible: individuals are perfectly capable of entering SCP-055's container and observing it, taking mental or written notes, making sketches, taking photographs, and even making audio/video recordings. An extensive log of such observations is on file. However, information about SCP-055's physical appearance "leaks" out of a human mind soon after such an observation. Individuals tasked with describing SCP-055 afterwards find their minds wandering and lose interest in the task; individuals tasked with sketching a copy of a photograph of SCP-055 are unable to remember what the photograph looks like, as are researchers overseeing these tests.*
>
> *...All of these facts are periodically rediscovered, usually by chance readers of this file, causing a great deal of alarm. This state of concern lasts minutes at most, before the matter is simply forgotten about.*

A fictional interview between "Dr. Hughes" and a classified personnel member begins as follows:[5]

> *Dr. Hughes: Okay, I'm going to need to ask you some questions about number 55 now.*
> *████████████: Number what?*
> *Dr. Hughes: SCP object 55. The object you just examined.*

---

4. "SCP-055," SCP Foundation Wiki, accessed December 20, 2024, https://scp-wiki.wikidot.com/scp-055.
5. Ibid.

███████████: *Um, I don't know what you're talking about. I don't think we have a 55.*
Dr. Hughes: *Okay, then,* ███████████, *I'd like you to tell me what you've been doing for the past two hours.*
███████████: *What? I... <subject appears uncomfortable> ... I don't know.*

SCP-055 formed the basis for a horror fiction book by qntm, called *There Is No Antimemetics Division* (often abbreviated to TINAD), which he published in 2021, several months before my ex-colleague recommended it to me in our email thread.[6]

I purchased and read TINAD in the fall of that year. Or, rather, I should say that, as a fan of Lovecraftian horror, I devoured it. It was spooky and disturbing in all the right ways. In qntm's world, antimemes were not an abstract concept, but live creatures that stalked through the pages of the book. Exploring antimemes in an unconstrained, fictional universe made it easier to consider how their underlying qualities might transfer to the real world.

Antimemes predate the internet's culture wars. Yet, despite the commercial success of qntm's book, they do not yet feature prominently in social media discourse, though a number of online communities engage with its concepts in quieter corners of the web. But, like the rise of group chats: timing is everything. TINAD brought the concept to a wider audience right around the time that people like I, and my ex-colleague, were searching for vocabulary to describe what was happening to the internet, and how ideas spread – or don't spread – in today's world.

Part of the appeal of antimemetics was not just its relevance to the cultural discourse, but my personal life. At the time, I was struggling to figure out what relationship I wanted to have with Twitter moving forward. Twitter had

---

6. "Antimemetics," SCP Database Wiki, accessed December 20, 2024, https://scp-db.fandom.com/wiki/Antimemetics.

been a huge part of my life, both personally and professionally. I had met some of my closest friends – even my spouse! – on there, and most of my work opportunities had come from Twitter, even if indirectly. Increasingly, however, I felt overwhelmed by the constant shouting and sketchy ads, along with a growing dread that the discourse had become more shallow and iterative. Without meaning to, I had begun my retreat, moving the conversations I used to have with friends on Twitter over to private channels.

In this embryonic, shielded version of my public self, my newsletter took on a new shine. I'd started a newsletter on TinyLetter (a platform acquired by email provider Mailchimp, and eventually shuttered) back in 2016 as an easy way to send email updates to subscribers about my latest writing. While the line I'd drawn around my world was mostly imaginary – anyone could read my public newsletter archive – I liked that it created an intimate, semi-private space for me and my readers. I preferred speaking to a room of a few thousand people who genuinely cared about what I had to say, instead of lobbing my ideas into the void of a hyper-public platform. Like giving a talk in a bookstore, anyone could drop in if they wanted, but the format made it clear that this was a place for me to hold a conversation with my intended audience, and that any new visitors would need to abide by our norms. On Twitter, such norms were nonexistent and nearly impossible to enforce.

This newsletter – which I eventually migrated to Substack – became my primary form of communication for several years. I loved sending out monthly issues and corresponding with everyone who thoughtfully replied. In many cases, I received useful feedback that helped inform my work – including the book you're reading now. After mentioning that I'd read TINAD in one of my newsletters, another blogger friend reached out via email. He had read it too, and had also told another friend to read it, who had then interviewed qntm about it. In what was, in retrospect, a classically antimemetic move, the three of us spun up an email thread to casually explore these concepts over the following year. Our dialogue contributed immensely to the ideas in this book.

Around the same time, it just so happened that I had been writing my first book, *Working in Public: The Making and Maintenance of Open Source Software*. I'd spent the prior few years researching how open source software – free and public code that anyone can use, ranging from hobby developers to big companies and institutions – was built. What I'd found defied the rosy picture that most people associated with open source: a crowdsourced effort driven by many volunteers, the way many people imagine Wikipedia is written (spoiler: it's not). After talking to hundreds of developers of popular open source projects, I learned that most projects were built by one or a few developers, many of whom faced burdensome demands for customer support, rather than contributions, from their users. Open, borderless communities were a recipe for entitlement, rather than collaboration.

This was an important point to highlight for the open source software industry itself, but – especially as *all* of social media seemed to be hurtling towards something equally chaotic and sinister, and perhaps for similar reasons – it was also impossible to ignore as an indictment of the free and open internet we'd been promised.

In the late 1990s, following the end of the Cold War and defeat of communism, optimists believed that Western liberal democracy had finally proven itself the most viable form of government. Political scientist Francis Fukuyama called it the "end of history" in 1989, theorizing that major ideological conflicts had been resolved, and that we were now entering a period of prolonged peace and stability. The early consumer internet, which emerged around the same time, symbolized the universal adoption of democratic principles. People believed that when ideas were allowed to spread unconstrained, our differences would blur, leaving behind only a shared camaraderie.

Around this time, open source software became a poster child of globalism. The story sold itself: a bunch of unaffiliated software developers, living around the world, working together to create and maintain software for public use. What's more, they did this not because it was profitable, but because they enjoyed it.

The reality that unfolded, however – lone, overworked developers, crushed under a flood of support requests from demanding users – was less appealing. Similarly, the idea that the internet would lead to a resolution of differences turned out to be overly optimistic. Instead, increased visibility into group differences *exacerbated* tribalism, which led to a vicious balkanization of the internet. I realized, while writing my book, that what had happened in open source was a harbinger of what was to come for everyone.

And that was why I went to work at Substack, cold DMing one of its founders on Twitter to plead my case, and eventually joining as its second employee in the fall of 2019. To most people in tech, Substack was still, if they'd heard of it at all, indistinguishable from Mailchimp, a service used primarily for sending marketing emails – you know, the kind that say, *"Fourth of July sale starts NOW! 25% off all items"* or *"Updates to our privacy policy."* At the time, Substack occupied a tiny, fluorescent-lit office in the Financial District of San Francisco, with a whiteboard covered in Post-Its that we used to plan priorities for the week.

I had been hired to help grow Substack's fledgling writer community, but I tried to make myself useful however I could, whether it was redesigning the homepage to be more writer-friendly or tackling our customer support queue. I couldn't explain why Substack wasn't just another Mailchimp, nor why it felt so important to me to work there. But it seemed like the web was tilted on its side, poised to flip from hyper-public to hyper-fiefdomed, and I wanted to help bring in the next era of online discourse.

Of course, I wasn't the only one who felt this way. Earlier that year, Kickstarter and Metalabel co-founder

Yancey Strickler – whom I eventually approached about publishing this book – had published a wildly popular essay titled "The Dark Forest Theory of the Internet." Strickler likened our changing digital landscape to a "dark forest" – borrowing a metaphor from Cixin Liu's *Three Body Problem* trilogy – in which an imagined forest is quiet, not because it is peaceful or devoid of activity, but because it is dangerous to reveal one's presence.[7] Any activity could only take place in safe, hidden spaces, away from predators who prowl through the forest. Venkatesh Rao, a writer and co-founder of the blog *Ribbonfarm*, built upon Strickler's dark forest metaphor by introducing the idea of the "cozyweb,"[8] which designer Maggie Appleton later summarized as "the private, gatekeeper-bounded spaces of the internet we have all retreated to over the last few years."[9] Though each used their own vocabulary to describe what was happening, it seemed that everyone was pointing to the same set of emerging dynamics that were shifting the very nature of online public discourse.

I SAT ON THE IDEAS you're now reading for nearly three years before deciding to write this book. Back in 2021, I had considered writing an essay about what I thought were the key concepts behind antimemetics, and why they mattered. But, like so many messy drafts before they become finished products, the ideas moved faster than I could keep up. I was slipping and sliding all over the place, writing down more and more examples that I came across, and cramming them into a big, braindumped doc called *antimemetics-notes.md*, which perched itself, mockingly, in the top-left corner of my desktop for years. Whenever I had some

---

7.   Yancey Strickler, "The Dark Forest Theory of the Internet," *Medium*, May 20, 2019, https://ystrickler.medium.com/the-dark-forest-theory-of-the-internet-7dc3e68a7cb1.
8.   Venkatesh Rao, "The Extended Internet Universe," *Contraptions*, May 24, 2019, https://contraptions.venkateshrao.com/p/the-extended-internet-universe.
9.   Maggie Appleton, "Cozy Web," *Maggie Appleton*, accessed December 20, 2024, https://maggieappleton.com/cozy-web.

downtime between projects, I would try to refine this doc into *antimemetics-draft.md*. Each time, I would get frustrated by its unwieldiness and set it aside again.

I had also convinced myself that this project was, somehow, not worth investing time into, or at least difficult to justify. A book about ideas? It was just so...abstract. So navel-gazey. So self-indulgent. I was, to be honest, somewhat disgusted with myself. I wanted to do things that felt real, tangible, and grounded in "actual" happenings in the world. I threw myself into a different book project – one that was heavy on stories, but light on theory.

In the summer of 2023, I hiked up a hill in San Francisco with a friend and his sweet, naughty Labrador retriever. While she strained at her leash, gobbling voraciously at every bit of trash on the sidewalk – a discarded soda cup, a half-eaten chicken leg – I confessed my frustration with the many hoops I had to jump through in order to write something that didn't even feel quite like "me." After getting feedback that the original versions were too academic-sounding and detailed, I had revised the proposal several times, editing all the bits of myself out until what remained was a perfectly well-behaved, inoffensive book that might be suitable for a general audience. The stories I had curated were unique to my perspective on the problem; that I knew. But the writing style felt like an imitation of my actual writing, aimed at giving publishers what they wanted to see. The thesis had strayed far from my initial perspective. What I had now was a simulacrum of a book, a symbol that stood in for a certain set of beliefs aimed at a certain type of person, but which contained few original ideas.

"But Nadia, this isn't right!" my friend exclaimed. He yanked on his puppy's leash, guiding her away – snorting and slobbering happily – from another piece of trash. "You should write about the things you actually care about. How can we resolve this?"

I explained my desire to focus on things that were "real" and "tangible." I confessed to feeling somewhat sheepish about my more abstract interests. "For example," I said, "there's a half-written draft I've had for several years now about this notion of antimemetics: ideas that are important, but that we can't seem to focus on or retain memory of." But, I explained, "that's a *way* too abstract topic that feels silly to write about."

My friend reminded me that one of my most popular essays to date is titled "The tyranny of ideas": a dashed-off piece about how ideas control us, not the other way around. It was true: I published that essay on my blog in 2019 without much thought. It was just a fun piece. But it's the piece that many people who've read my work will tell me they first discovered. Similarly, a longer essay that I published in 2022, called "Idea machines" – no relationship to the 2019 essay, except that both were about the nature of ideas – mapped out how ideas turn into outcomes, complete with schematic diagrams. That essay, too, I had been somewhat embarrassed to publish, because it seemed so abstract. Yet, that essay also seemed to have an enduring popularity, with practical applications for people interested in movement building.

What I've finally come to understand is that how we think directly influences how we act. Though this may sound obvious, it is not widely believed in practice. Even my ex-colleague, in his initial email to me about memetics engineering research, explained his interest in "the types of thoughts that have huge effects on thinking (as opposed to effects on action, I guess?)". Memes have gotten politicians elected, amplified wars and uprisings, and influenced how we talk to each other and which ideas we choose to spend our time and money on. Why were antimemes any less interesting or important to try to understand?

The impetus to finally write this book came from the Dark Forest Collective, a veritable league of superheroes – including the aforementioned Strickler, Rao, and Appleton – that came to my poor abandoned project's rescue. The Dark Forest Collective had just published an anthology about the changing social web, and they were looking for related ideas to bring to life. What had once felt too "navel-gazey" to me in the context of memetic public discourse – where one must jostle for likes and retweets – felt perfectly right for the audience they had curated. It's why I finally decided to publish the book you're holding in your hands.

Finding the confidence to write this book depended, ironically, on me finding just the right antimemetic environment to hold and nourish these ideas. And although I hope you enjoy and get some value out of this book, I confess that I undertook this project more for me than for you. Plenty has been written already about whether culture is stagnant or even dead; about whether we are trapped in the Dark Ages of creativity, forever recycling the fresh ideas that were minted in prior decades. Creative self-expression is the only way we will continue to make our mark as humans in times of uncertainty, and it doesn't come from doing what you think will sell to other people. It comes from wanting to express something deep in your soul. Sometimes those ideas are trite and "cringe," and most of them fail to find an audience. But we can't let this fear of failure keep us from trying to produce things that feel truly original to us. It is precisely these fears that keep us trapped in a holding pattern, where every artifact produced is always for the approval of someone else.

My hope for you, however, is that as you read this book, you'll not only see the world through a new lens, but find your own role in navigating the antimemetic forces that shape it. In the chapters ahead, we'll explore antimemetics from every angle: how they emerge, how they work, and how we can work with these forces to accomplish interesting things.

Chapter 1 introduces antimemetics by contrasting it with memetics – how ideas spread – and in the context of *mimetic behavior*, or René Girard's theory of imitative desire. We look at how memetics came to govern our modern world, and how antimemetics emerged as a quiet counter-force to its excesses.

Chapter 2 breaks down the mechanics of antimemetic spread – using concepts like immunity, transmission rate, and symptomatic periods – to show how ideas move from taboo to acceptance within a network.

Chapter 3 dives into the broader evolutionary dynamics of ideas. We look at how memes, antimemes, and supermemes are forged in the dense, isolated networks of the modern internet, and how different types of ideas shape our cultural ecosystems.

In *Chapter 4*, we zoom into the individual, or node level of networks. I argue that attention is the key ingredient that shapes not just our personal realities, but also determines which ideas we collectively embrace or reject.

Chapters 5 and 6 move us from theory to practice. In Chapter 5, I explore how ideas are, or can be made, intentionally obscure, and how truth-tellers bring them to light. In Chapter 6, we look at how to keep antimemes at the forefront of our minds, and how champions make sure we don't forget.

Antimemes have always existed, but – like memes in the 2010s – our present cultural moment creates a "living laboratory" to better examine them in action. Unpacking these dynamics can help us understand the contemporary political, social, and cultural disruptions we're embroiled in. But it also reveals new layers to the underlying "physics" of ideas and how they spread, and the role that each of us can play in making progress on important topics.

HIDDEN CITY

1

CHINA MIÉVILLE'S *THE CITY & THE CITY* chronicles the fictional story of two cities, Besźel and Ul Qoma, which exist in the same physical location. Their citizens live in a state of perpetual cognitive dissonance, having been trained from birth to "unsee," or ignore, the people, buildings, and events in the other city. They live, eat, work, and sleep in parallel societies, never noticing that the other exists. This tacit social agreement is enforced by a shadowy organization, known as Breach, whose members are permitted to perceive both cities and watch for transgressions. For all other residents, acknowledging the other city is considered a serious crime.

Today, we live in our own version of *The City & The City*: two different societies, governed by memetic and antimemetic forces, which operate in tandem, yet are rarely acknowledged by the other.

The *memetic city* is easily recognizable. It is the realm of viral ideas and social contagion: tweets that explode overnight, social media avatars supporting the latest political cause, TikToks and Instagram Reels that we scroll through at the end of a long day. Here, ideas spread with lightning speed – amplified by social platforms – and shape our collective behavior and preferences: the opinions we hold, the dates we go on, who we vote for. Like Tokyo's Shibuya district or New York City's Times Square, the memetic city is vibrant, noisy, and undeniably culturally influential. It thrives on visibility; its power is rooted in the ability of ideas to quickly capture our attention and replicate across the hive mind.

But the strength and might of the memetic city depends partly upon another, less visible, but equally powerful world that we don't always notice or see: the *antimemetic city*.

The antimemetic city resists replication, dwelling in the shadows of our collective consciousness. Like Shenzhen, which drives the global electronics market, or Zürich, which drives global finance, the antimemetic city is not

The memetic city of Tokyo's Shibuya district...

Image source: Flickr, via user nakashi. Uploaded December 12, 2018, licensed under CC BY-SA 2.0. https://flickr.com/photos/nakashi/45562277694/.

...compared to the antimemetic Zürich.

Image source: Flickr, via user IMBiblio. Uploaded December 22, 2015, licensed under CC BY-SA 2.0. https://flickr.com/photos/33750036@N05/23904933755/.

invisible for lack of importance, but because it thrives on operating quietly in the background.

In this city, we Google, ask ChatGPT, or browse Reddit for answers to questions we can't ask our friends or coworkers – *am I gay? do I make a lot of money? should I break up with my partner?* Tabs erupt across the top of our browser window like an algae bloom, only to be abandoned and rediscovered the next morning with a bewildered look and a head shake: "What was I *doing* last night?" We read links that are too fiery to discuss on public feeds, so we share them in our group chats instead. We tumble down YouTube rabbit holes, peering deeper into the abyss, until we find ourselves caught in the crosshairs of a stranger who is ranting and raving about frogs or tankies or the longhouse or nazbols – obscure online microtrends that never quite break into the mainstream. We subscribe to newsletters about things we're too embarrassed to tell others we want to know about: *COVID conspiracy theories, what women really think, my self-help journey to eternal bliss*.

It's tempting to classify some of these ideas as memetic, given how they transfix certain, smaller communities. But what makes these ideas antimemetic is how they propagate: in semi-private settings. You don't bring these ideas up at work, or at the family dinner table. Most people don't post about these things from their main social media accounts. Antimemetic ideas resist the spotlight, drawing eager listeners into darker corners of the internet, rather than the neon, broadcasted feeds of the memetic city. These ideas flourish precisely because they live under the radar.

Antimemetics are a shadow city built on thoughts, knowledge, and practices that do not spread easily, despite their importance to our lives. It is a place where lost wisdom, suppressed beliefs, and uncomfortable truths circulate freely, only to be forgotten once we return to the bright, sunny memetic city. In the antimemetic world, ideas move slowly but deliberately; their integrity is protected from the relentless, compressed cycle of memetic replication.

Thus far, the history of the Digital Age has been written by the memeologists. Everyone knows what a meme is; that social media made it possible for ideas to "go viral" much more easily than before; and that this sort of virality fundamentally changed how our politics, media, and culture evolve and spread.

But as our online landscape is increasingly saturated with memetics, a second narrative has come into sharper relief. Antimemetics are just as old as memetics, but they've only become perceptible as people seek refuge from memetic overload: an overwhelming barrage of ideas replicating, peaking, and dying at the speed of light. Memes, too, predate the internet, but became more visible after social media sped up their rate of transmission. An ant crawling across a floorboard is less noticeable than a fly zipping through the air.

Antimemes, by their very nature, pass through our social filters undetected. They tend to influence us in subtler ways. But we can learn a lot about ourselves, and the networks we operate in, by examining not just what we share, but what we withhold – and why.

MEMES WANT TO BE SHARED. When we come across a particularly good meme, our first instinct is to pass it on to someone else. Memes reap the benefits of these urges by spreading rapidly from person to person – like a virus – and burying themselves into our respective cultures.

Antimemes are the opposite. When we encounter an antimemetic object, there is a reflexive desire – consciously or not – to suppress it. Antimemetic ideas are constantly being rediscovered, but are either forgotten soon after they are encountered, or are invisible to perception altogether. (Remember the fictional Dr. Hughes' notes on SCP-055.)

It is not that antimemes are boring or uninteresting. Legal contracts, for example, or mathematical proofs, are not really antimemetic. They are difficult for most of us to comprehend or engage with, but this is because they are dense and complex to work through. Antimemes, on the other hand, are objects that you *want* to remember – in the moment, you found them quite compelling – but don't seem to stick in your memory beyond a short duration.

This sort of forgetfulness shows up frequently in our personal behavior. There are actions we know we should prioritize, but can't seem to keep top of mind. Consider a relationship or job that makes you miserable, but you can't seem to quit, because when things are good, you can't remember why they were ever bad. Many people also can't seem to prioritize behaviors like eating well and exercising regularly, or saving for retirement, even though they know they ought to. Cognitive biases, too, like Gell-Mann amnesia (where we recognize that the media reports inaccurately on topics we know well, yet trust their expertise on topics we don't) or the Baader-Meinhof phenomenon (noticing a word or concept everywhere once we've been made aware of it), have antimemetic qualities.

But this sort of cognitive dissonance on a personal level bubbles up to the collective, too. Truths that are too heavy or consequential, such as the existence of global poverty or human trafficking, struggle to remain at the forefront of our minds. Natural disaster prevention is significantly cheaper than fixing damage caused by disasters later, but it is frequently deprioritized within government budgets.[10] Mass shootings trigger predictable media cycles in which politicians and advocates call for increased gun safety legislation, only to be abandoned when the hype fades. Financial bubbles are driven not just by herd mentality, but antimemetic as well: when markets are at their peak, eager investors tend to forget that what goes up will

---

10. Federal Emergency Management Agency (FEMA), *Natural Hazard Mitigation Saves: An Independent Study to Assess the Future Savings from Mitigation Activities*, accessed December 20, 2024, https://www.fema.gov/sites/default/files/2020-07/mitigationsaves_poster16x20_180611.pdf.

Oroville Dam, the tallest dam in the United States, located in California. In 2017, heavy rainfalls caused severe damage which required the evacuation of 180,000 residents nearby. Authorities were criticized for not taking adequate steps to maintain the dam and manage risks of failure.

Image source: Flickr, via user caguard. Uploaded on Febuary 25, 2017, licensed under CC BY 2.0. https://flickr.com/photos/caguard/33071623756/.

eventually come back down, despite decades of historical data.

Both memes and antimemes have existed for thousands of years. I don't want to assume what you already know, so I'll start with a short history of memes, which will help orient us to the world of antimemes. (If you're already a certified memeologist who's familiar with this history, feel free to skip ahead to the next section.)

Memes are, at their core, ideas wrapped in lightweight packages, which enable them to propagate through societies, and often reinforce shared values. *Symbols* (like the Christian cross), *customs* and *rituals* (such as handshakes or a thumbs-up gesture), and *aphorisms* ("Actions speak louder than words," "Don't bite the hand that feeds you") are all examples of ideas that spread memetically, long before the advent of the internet.

Richard Dawkins coined the term "meme" in his 1976 book *The Selfish Gene* to describe self-replicating cultural objects that spread and evolve like biological genes. A "memeplex" is the institutionalized version of a meme, referring to a *group* of memes – such as a religion or political party – that reinforce each other via replication.

With the birth of the consumer internet in the late 1990s – accelerated by the social platforms that followed – memes suddenly became a much more visible phenomenon. Email, internet forums, and early social platforms like YouTube made it easier to share bite-sized ideas, and these ideas were elevated to a fame and prominence of their own. I remember watching an episode of *South Park*, aired in 2008, where early internet stars – Numa Numa, Star Wars Kid, Sneezing Panda – gather at the Colorado Department of Internet Money, waiting to collect their checks for their viral videos. It is quaint to remember a time in which we had less than ten viral internet sensations to keep track of.

Memes eventually became associated with more than stupid internet humor, as ideas of all kinds began using the same distribution channels to replicate more quickly.

Starting in the late 2000s, memes drove *political campaigns* (Barack Obama's 2008 presidential campaign was heavily lauded for its use of social media), *revolutions* (Arab Spring activists used Facebook and Twitter to coordinate their efforts), *terrorism* (ISIS, the decentralized foil to its top-down predecessor, Al-Qaeda, was the first major terrorist group to use social media for recruiting and propaganda), and *information warfare* (foreign and domestic actors notoriously spread misinformation in 2016 in order to influence the U.S. presidential election). And that's when things started to get weird.

Dawkins' work explains cultural transmission from the perspective of memes themselves, but he has less to say about what *motivates* their spread, from the view of carriers – in other words, *us*. Dawkins treats carriers as a more passive, instrumental role, when he discusses them at all; memes are the ones who find ways to survive and replicate, and we're just part of the landscape.

For our purposes, however, if we are to understand why ideas *don't* always spread through a network, our investigation must include a closer look at carrier motivations. I will now invoke the name that all certified memeologists have been waiting patiently to hear: René Girard, a French historian who first described these interpersonal dynamics through the lens of mimetic desire in the 1960s. (Note that this is *mimetics* with an "i" – referring to mimicry, or imitation – not an "e," as in Dawkins' *memes*.)

Girard believes that humans are governed not by intrinsic personal preferences, but aspirational "models," towards which we unconsciously orient our behavior. In Girard's framework, desire is formed from the balance of three positions. There is a *subject* (the person who wants something) and an *object* (the thing they want). But most compelling is the *model*, or the person that the subject wishes to imitate, through their desire of the object. As Girard sees it, we crave certain objects not because we actually want them, but because other people – the models

— do. But when these objects are scarce or limited — for example, two people wanting the same promotion at work — competing for the same things can lead to rivalry and conflict.

To resolve this tension, Girard argues, communities resort to *scapegoating* – think witch hunts, or cancel culture – where an individual or group is singled out, blamed for the conflict, and expelled, or "sacrificed," to restore harmony. The scapegoat absorbs the community's aggression and provides a common enemy to unite its members, which reestablishes social order. Girard believes this cycle – widespread mimetic desire, which leads to rivalry, and is then resolved through scapegoating – is foundational to human culture and explains much of historical violence and conflict, from the French Revolution in the 1700s to Rwandan genocide in the 1990s.

Mimetic desire might not fully explain why *every* type of meme, à la Dawkins, is propagated. Some memes, for example, are passed along because simply we find them entertaining, or we want to strengthen relationships with the person we pass them onto – though this, too, could be recast in the light of modeling ourselves after those we look up to. But mimetic desire is one way to understand why many memes, such as fashion trends, political opinions, or slang take off. People replicate them because they are imitating a memeplex – a political philosophy, a trendy subculture, a desirable way of life.

If we take this behavior as canon and pour a bottle of fuel over it, we can then understand why the internet, rather than ushering in an era of global peace, made us leap at each other's throats. The root of human conflict has not just political and cultural origins, but psychological ones, as well. Our collective belief in democracy, no matter how strong, failed to singlehandedly override our baser mimetic desires.

Social platforms – Twitter, Instagram, Facebook, Snap, TikTok, YouTube – not only exposed us to more models of desire at unprecedented scale, but encouraged competition by doling out cheap rewards: likes, shares, followers. Like any population exposed to a highly addictive substance for the first time, we were wholly unequipped to handle this level of mimetic desire in our lives.

Some people have declared a more ominous version of Fukuyama's end of history: a sort of Dark Age where culture is merely recycled, rather than created. This cultural stasis, if it is real, appears to be a product of memetic overgrowth, like a yeast that's buried itself into every warm, dark corner of our minds and allowed its white spores to unfurl. Culture critic Ted Gioia, a proponent of the Dark Age thesis, points out that only 27% of music tracks streamed today are new or recent; that 83% of Hollywood revenues come from franchise films; that increasingly, the most popular video games – *Minecraft*, *Grand Theft Auto*, *Super Mario Bros* – are old; and that these trends are accelerating. "We will soon enter an era," Gioia writes, "when children will play versions of the same games that their *grandparents* once enjoyed."[11]

W. David Marx, who bridges mimetic desire and cultural production in his book, *Status and Culture*, argues that the value of cultural goods like music, fashion, and art usually derives not from their intrinsic merits, but the social status they confer. While social media made it easier to discover and access new, ever-more niche subcultures, Marx believes it also reduced our desire to challenge culture in surprising ways, because it's more prestigious – by mimetic standards – to use proven formulas for grabbing people's attention than to do something potentially risky and original.

Mimetic behavior *does* rule the world now: from politics, to art, to friendships and relationships. The consumer internet, along with social platforms and smartphones built on top of it, created the ideal environment for

---

11. Ted Gioia, "Why Do I Keep Saying the Culture is Stagnating?" *The Honest Broker*, August 30, 2023, https://www.honest-broker.com/p/why-do-i-keep-saying-the-culture.

mimetic desire to grow unconstrained. As memes dominate our lives, we've fully embraced our role as carriers, reorienting our behavior and identities towards emulating the most powerful – and often the most primal and base – models of desire. Taken to the extreme, this could be seen as a horrifying loss of human capacity to build and create in new and surprising ways.

Even if mimetic desire is an accurate description of human behavior, however, it doesn't give us much hope for the future. It seems depressing to simply resign ourselves to this sort of relentlessly competitive behavior, with no recourse for the future, until our brains melt or the universe implodes. I would like to believe that humans are a little bit smarter than that – or, if nothing else, that memes are indeed as selfish as Dawkins claims, and that as we develop immunity to the most common memes, the weirder ones – those that genuinely surprise us, shock us, make us joyful, make us feel *some*thing real – will find ways to reproduce even in an inhospitable environment.

Let us choose to believe that our civilization will not simply break down into savagery, competition, and global conflict as we slide towards a destructive end. Let us choose to believe that we are not reverting back to a state of primitivism. Mimetic desire might explain how we got here, but as we search for ways to survive, it is a second, hidden set of behaviors – antimemetic ones – that will show us how to move forward. Let's rewind our history of the Digital Age and start again: this time from the perspective of the unseen, shadow city.

ONCE AGAIN, I TURN TO China Miéville for his brilliant, evocative imagery – this time, from his novel *Embassytown*, published shortly after *The City & The City*.

Embassytown depicts a fictional town of the same name, whose native species, the Ariekei, use a special form of language. Their language is literal – they have no concept of metaphors or analogies – and must be spoken with two words at a time, instead of one. Humans cannot speak their language, except for twins who are bred for this purpose and serve as "Ambassadors."

When a new Ambassador, Ez/Ra, comes to town – comprised, for the first time, of two people who are *not* twins – the Ariekei become addicted to their speech, which sounds different compared to what twins can produce. What starts as an amusing novelty gives way to obsession as the residents' lives fall to pieces. The Ariekei begin wandering the streets like zombies, tearing the world apart in search of more "god-drug."

Thankfully, a small band of Ariekei manages to free themselves of addiction and develop a more nuanced, alternative language, which includes the concept of metaphors. This new language becomes the solution to their problems after an Embassytown resident introduces it to the Ariekei. Armed with a new ability to express complex thoughts, the Arikei find that Ez/Ra's voice has lost its addictive power. They are free to move forward, connecting to the outside world in deeper and more sophisticated ways than before.

Just like the memes, antimemes have been here all along, working their hidden magic throughout history. *Taboos* (such as discussing sex, politics, or finances), *open secrets* ("Don't ask, don't tell"), *whisper networks* (such as the Underground Railroad), *secret societies* (such as the Freemasons or Illuminati), and *hidden languages* (such as graffiti) are all ways in which important ideas spread through private channels. But if the mid-2000s were the point where memes took off, the late 2010s marked the point that antimemes began to emerge as a counterforce to memetic overload.

At first, memetic growth fostered a rich diversity of subcultures, enabling us – like a newly anointed mantis shrimp, who can perceive colors with twelve photoreceptors, compared to humans' three – to perceive a more complex spectrum of values, politics, and interests than mainstream media channels had previously permitted. Movements like Black Lives Matter and the Tea Party cracked open their respective political bases, revealing a constellation of political subcultures. Gamergate, social justice warriors, QAnon, and anarcho-primitivists all emerged from the woods, looked around, and spotted each other.

We had entered, briefly, the era of "memetic tribes," a term coined by Peter Limberg in 2018 to refer to this rapid speciation of internet-first subcultures. Limberg defines memetic tribes as "a group of agents with a meme complex...that directly or indirectly seeks to impose its distinct map of reality – along with its moral imperatives – on others."[12]

Operating in full view on social platforms, and egged on by the rewards of saying increasingly outrageous, attention-grabbing, and polarizing things online, these tribes began to acquire more members through public signaling. Instead of red tribes and blue tribes, there was now a multitude of memetic tribes, each with "competing claims, interests, goals, and organizations":

> *An establishment leftist who squabbles with the right must contend with mockery from the Dirtbag Left. Meanwhile, the Dirtbag Left endures critiques from Social Justice Activists (SJA), who in turn are criticized by the Intellectual Dark Web (IDW). The trench warfare of the old culture war has become an all-out brawl.*

As Girard would have told us, these tribes began squabbling over a scarce resource: public mindshare. As the wars raged on, their mimetic rivalry gave way to scapegoating, formalized as "cancel culture." Countless people were fired

---

12.   Connor Barnes and Peter Limberg, "Memetic Tribes and Culture War 2.0," *Medium*, September 13, 2018, https://medium.com/s/world-wide-wtf/memetic-tribes-and-culture-war-2-0-14705c43f6bb.

from their jobs, or ostracized from society, for transgressions pushed under the microscope of the public web. Every time someone, or some group, was scapegoated, it helped bring the accusing group's members closer together. *Marginal Revolution* blogger Tyler Cowen calls "Big Tech (most of all Facebook)" the "Girardian sacrifice for the Trump victory in 2016."[13]

But the proliferation of memetic tribes strained the core assumptions underpinning Girard's framework, as context collapse made it impossible for any one scapegoat – no matter how big – to fully resolve conflicts *between* tribes. One tribe's scapegoat was another's hero, and the act of scapegoating, or being scapegoated, even became itself a mimetic model to aspire to.

When Girard developed his theory of mimetic desire, he was living in a world where there was only one major public narrative to keep track of. Girard passed away in 2015; he didn't live to see what social media matured into. Today, that shared public narrative has mostly dissolved. There are now thousands of microsocieties budding and bursting in months or weeks, with many of us occupying multiple societies simultaneously. Scapegoating doesn't explain how we finally managed to exit the dreadful loop of the 2010s culture wars. It only explains how we became trapped in a state of perpetual warfare – what Strickler called the "dark forest" – in the first place.

But we did manage to exit this dreadful loop, somehow, though it required a different path. Some dissenters quietly unhanded themselves of addictive god-drug and set out to find a better way of living. Private fortresses dotted the horizon, perched among the distant prairies of the web. Memetic tribes, who now reserved their public behavior for deliberate warfare or recruitment, occasionally popped

---

13.   Tyler Cowen, "The changes in vibes — why did they happen?," *Marginal Revolution*, July 17, 2024, https://marginalrevolution.com/marginalrevolution/2024/07/the-changes-in-vibes-why-did-they-happen.html.

their heads out the trenches to shoot or return fire to another tribe.

If the memetic city is characterized by bright, flashy Times Square, the antimemetic city is more like a city of encampments, strewn across an interminable desert. While some camps are bigger and more storied – think long-established internet forums, private social clubs, or Discords – its primary social unit is the group chat, which makes it easy to instantly throw up four walls around any conversation online.

Group chats, as a concept, are a perfect example of the self-censoring nature of antimemes. They are rarely discussed by mainstream media outlets, because, unlike public platforms like Twitter and Reddit, which provide endless content mining opportunities for eager journalists, there is nothing to write about with group chats. Occasionally, a piece about group chats finds its way to *The New York Times* or *The Atlantic*, but these stories are usually quaint and rosy, reflecting on the joys of drinking wine with one's college girlfriends, or keeping in touch with old colleagues, rather than how they will reshape the online social web.

And yet, as journalist Sophie Haigney writes in *The New York Times*, group chats have clearly replaced "backroom meetings among powerful media figures" as the modern successor to "the proverbial smoke-filled room."[14] Somewhere out there, your favorite celebrities and politicians and executives are tapping away on their keyboards in a Signal or Telegram or Whatsapp chat, planning campaigns and revolutions and corporate takeovers. (Haigney, for her part, tells us that she uses her preferred group chat, "The Girls," to recap her Friday nights from bed.) No journalist has access to the most influential group chats, and

---

14. Sophie Haigney, "How Group Chats Rule the World," *The New York Times Magazine*, January 16, 2024, https://www.nytimes.com/2024/01/16/magazine/group-chats.html.

those who do cannot write about them, or else risk losing their membership. The secrets keep themselves.

Leaks do happen. *The New Republic*'s Ken Silverstein, for example, published an exposé of a group chat called Off-Leash, started by military contractor Erik Prince, in which government officials and denizens of the Washington, D.C. swamp speculated on Israeli-Palestinian relations and how to overthrow the Iranian regime.[15] Haigney reminds us of an article published in *The Australian Financial Review*, which alleged that FTX founder Sam Bankman-Fried had a group chat called "Wirefraud." Whether the chat is real or not, she reminds us, "it's funny how easy it is to imagine it being true: Where else would a group of tech people coordinate fraud but in the chat?"

ON APRIL 30, 2019, Meta (then Facebook) CEO Mark Zuckerberg took the stage at his company's annual developer conference and made a surprising declaration: "The future is private." His speech was an expansion of a post he'd published a month earlier, in which he observed that "private messaging, ephemeral stories, and small groups are by far the fastest growing areas of online communication." Moving forward, Zuckerberg said that Meta would prioritize these areas over Web 2.0 mainstays like public posts and the News Feed.

It is tempting to imagine these two cities – memetic and antimemetic – at war with each other, battling for our attention. But just like Miéville's imagined cities of Besźel and Ul Qoma, they are remarkable not because they are in conflict, but because they somehow manage to co-exist.

Although they offer temporary relief, group chats aren't a replacement for the hyperspeed of public platforms. Group chats serve as a safe space to experiment with our half-formed thoughts – *for* the public stage. Ven-

---

15. Ken Silverstein, "Off Leash: Inside the Secret, Global, Far-Right Group Chat," *The New Republic*, May 30, 2024, https://newrepublic.com/article/182008/erik-prince-secret-global-group-chat-off-leash.

ture capitalist Sriram Krishnan compares them to "a standup comic workshopping his set in a small club before a big Netflix special," while journalist Hannah Sung appreciates how "in the apocalyptic landscape of our algorithmically juiced culture wars, a group chat is a refuge where my ideas and thoughts don't have to be fully formed and battle ready. We grant one another a little grace, even when discussing polarizing topics such as defunding the police or the high cost of housing."[16, 17]

Group chats are a place to build trust with likeminded people, who eventually amplify each others' ideas in public settings. Memetic and antimemetic cities depend on each other: the stronger memes become, the more we need private spaces to refine them. Just as in the offline world, we have public streets and private homes, our online world now has public feeds and private chats. After the cities came the suburbs – we didn't just escape to the countryside.

Rohit Krishnan, who writes the newsletter *Strange Loop Canon*, posits that culture is downstream of the shape of our networks. Sparse networks, like public social platforms, are good at diffusing ideas quickly. Dense networks, like group chats, are better at reinforcing and strengthening ideas.[18] The same idea, disseminated across two different types of networks, leads people to exhibit different types of behavior.

Krishnan cites a 2015 paper from researchers Se Jung Park, Yon Soo Lim, and Han Woo Park, who examined the Occupy Wall Street movement as it spread through a wide, sparse network – Twitter – versus a dense, highly clustered one – YouTube, whose structure more closely

16. Sriram Krishnan, "Group chats rule the world," *Sriram Krishnan*, May 19, 2024, https://sriramk.com/group-chats-rule-the-world.
17. Hannah Sung, "The Last Place Left Online for Real Conversation," *The New York Times*, August 13, 2022, https://www.nytimes.com/2022/08/13/opinion/group-chats-social-media.html.
18. Rohit Krishnan, "Seeing Like a Network," *Strange Loop Canon*, June 19, 2024, https://www.strangeloopcanon.com/p/seeing-like-a-network.

resembles group chats today (or what they called a "small-world network").[19] The researchers found that influential voices on Twitter helped to disseminate information and bridge *across* communities, whereas those on YouTube had a high overlap in shared ideas and meanings. Both networks helped spread the ideas behind Occupy Wall Street, but in mutually reinforcing ways: Twitter by exposing the uninitiated to new ideas, and YouTube by reinforcing beliefs within existing members.

Without the content acquired from public platforms, group chats would have little to discuss. Even group chats that more closely resemble Haigney's "The Girls" – whose primary purpose is social bonding, not taking down governments – versus Prince's "Off-Leash" benefit from the articles, videos, and posts that fly around on public channels. Private spaces are where we get to refine ideas and strengthen relationships, but public spaces are the highway where those ideas zip around in hopes of being adopted and, eventually, brought to life in the physical world.

Antimemes didn't destroy memes: they just revealed a new layer of complexity to how memes are incubated. As anyone who's hoped for the demise of Twitter or Facebook has discovered, there is no foreseeable future in which all our online public spaces disappear – any more than it would make sense to do away with cities because we have suburbs. Our private and public spaces, as well as our online and offline spaces, are all intertwined. Or, as Haigney crisply put it: "Chat shapes life and life shapes chat."

WHILE THE ANTIMEMETIC CITY remains largely hidden from the memetic one, the two cities' proximity to each other, and the cross-cultural exchange that's ensued, gave

---

10. Se Jung Park et al., "Comparing Twitter and YouTube networks in information diffusion: The case of the 'Occupy Wall Street' movement," *Technological Forecasting and Social Change* vol. 95 (2019): 208-217, https://doi.org/10.1016/j.techfore.2015.02.003.

rise to new modes of interaction that contain characteristics of both places.

Peter Limberg chronicled the shift from "meme consciousness to vibe consciousness" in 2023 as a followup to his memetic tribes essay, titled "Meme to Vibe."[20] Vibes, he thinks, are "an evolutionary [adaptation] to the cartoonish gaslighting levels we face." Unlike memes, vibes are not legible, and are therefore much harder to track – but this is by design: "Vibes are about experiencing, not replicating."

Vibes combine the qualities of both memes and antimemes. They can still spread memetically (consider the effortless cool of "Parisian chic," or the ineffable warmth of "hygge"), but they are innately difficult to define, like an antimeme. They afford us the privacy to explore an idea's underlying premises more authentically and intimately than we otherwise could.

Vibes are like the sun: we know that they exist, but we can't ever look at them directly. Concepts like *community*, *mentorship*, *love*, *happiness*, *culture*, *education*, *progress*, and *paradigms* are similarly resistant to hard definitions. Like the sun, we can feel their warmth, see them skittering around the periphery of our vision...but most of us know never to acknowledge them head-on. And this is the way it should be, because defining them more precisely – a community platform; a mentor matching network; a happiness score – inevitably destroys their essence. It's not that we have failed to define them; it's that they are innately undefinable. To quote comedian Mitch Hedberg on why no one has been able to photograph Bigfoot:

> *I think Bigfoot is blurry. That's the problem...There's a large, out-of-focus monster roaming the countryside. Run, he's fuzzy, get out of here!*

20. Peter Limberg, "Meme to Vibe: A Philosophical Report," *Less Foolish*, March 6, 2023, https://lessfoolish.substack.com/p/meme-to-vibe-a-philosophical-report.

Even though we can only communicate these concepts tacitly, using metaphors and personal experience, this doesn't mean they are any less impactful on our lives. To try to make these ideas more specific is to miss the point. Societies function *better* when they have a category of ideas that escape precise definition, because ideas that can be measured can be controlled, or even exploited. We keep them imprecise to protect their integrity, splashing around together in the bathtub of blurry. No one can perfectly engineer a community, or love, or culture. Our most cherished ideas are kept safely out of the hands of those who want to play God.

It is unsurprising, then, that vibes gained special prominence in the Dark Forest era. Shortly before Limberg published his report, a group of people on Twitter decided to organize a "multiday ingroup festival" that became a sort of homage to vibes. But who was the ingroup in question? A defining trait of Vibecamp was that it explicitly resisted tribal affiliations. Its organizers – who are loosely affiliated with an online subculture called tpot, or "This Part of Twitter" – repeatedly use "ingroup" as a way of describing their aesthetic, but don't ever mention who the ingroup actually is. The ingroup is whomever affiliates with the ingroup, and it might contain people from many different ingroups. "This Part of Twitter" is, you know. *This* part of Twitter. (If none of this makes any sense, that's the point.)

Several hundred people attended the first Vibecamp. Despite being organized under "extremely online" circumstances, hardly anyone had their phones out at the festival; barely any photos were taken. While Brooke Bowman, one of Vibecamp's organizers, had originally imagined the event to be more like a traditional convention – with speakers, workshops, and booths – they ended up planning a much more informal gathering once they realized that, "Twitter wanted to just vibe."[21] There was a widespread, unspoken respect for attendees' anonymity and, in Bowman's words, "leaving the digital behind." Since then, Vibecamp has established itself as a permanent organization to facilitate annual gatherings, as well as smaller themed events throughout the year.

Vibecamp's manifesto, which is published on their website, calls for us to break "the atomized confines of digital modernity."[22] While the manifesto is broken out into "memes we live by," the memes themselves are profoundly antimemetic, as they emphasize the importance of embracing the unknowable and undefinable. "In a world that flattens people into caricatures," they write, "we choose to marvel at the kaleidoscopic swirl of stories animating every human." "In the age of echo chambers, we champion the disagreeable misfits who sincerely stand up for themselves and their ideas."

Vibecamp might be thought of as a spiritual successor to the digital detoxers of the 2010s, who tried to free themselves from the online world by turning off their phones and laptops and grounding themselves in offline interactions. While this approach worked for a day or a weekend-long retreat, the movement ultimately succumbed to practical constraints, as it became difficult to hold down a job, friendships, and relationships without a phone or laptop. And, of course, the offline world became so intertwined with the online world that it became impossible to escape its secondhand influence in the form of slang, fashion trends, pop culture figures, and political topics.

Vibecampers are taking a less drastic approach: embracing online public spaces, while still encouraging us to find what is true to each of us individually, rather than

---

21. Brooke Bowman and Alex Grin, "Vibecamp: Looking Forward w/ Brooke Bowman & Alex Grin," moderated by Peter Limberg, posted June 22, 2022, by The Stoa, YouTube, https://www.youtube.com/watch?v=cuaRBuES0x0.
22. Rob Hardy, "Memes We Live By," *Vibecamp*, accessed December 20, 2024, https://vibe.camp/.

mindlessly parroting others' behavior. But both movements are products of their respective cultural moments. They point towards a deeper collective yearning, even if all of us don't engage with their premises as seriously. Its members want us to remind us what we are at risk of losing; to not forget what else we could be.

WE ARE NOW LIVING IN what might be termed "late-stage memetic society" but "early-stage antimemetic society": a patchwork of settlements that has opened its borders to refugees fleeing memetic contagion. But the culture wars – while serving as proof of antimemes' growing importance – only offer a sociological explanation for why they have suddenly appeared in our lives. To understand where the world is going next, we need to go one level deeper into the fundamental mechanics of antimemes.

DRAG
COEFFICIENT

2

AT THE DAWN OF WEB 2.0, when every consumer product wanted to leverage its user base to "go viral," growth marketers used something called K-factor to track viral spread:

$$K = i * c$$

where i = number of invites sent by a customer, and c = conversion rate. If someone invited 10 of their friends to join Instagram, for example, and 20% of them joined, their K-factor would be 2.

Marketers borrowed this formula from epidemiology, which includes the study of how actual diseases spread. Viruses with a K-factor of 1 are stable (neither growing nor declining), while a K-factor of >1 indicates exponential growth.

Implicit in growth marketers' love of K-factor was the belief that *more virality = good*. If virality is the goal, this number ought to be as high as possible. But in the Dark Forest era, virality is no longer automatically considered desirable. If an idea spreads too quickly, it might escape its original context; its meaning could become distorted, and pushback could be so strong that it destroys the idea altogether. To find the ideal rate of transmission, then, we must therefore consider not only how *easily* an idea is transmitted, but the *immunity*, or resistance, of the network in which it operates.

In his interactive essay "Going Critical," writer and software engineer Kevin Simler offers a helpful introduction to visualizing how ideas spread through a social network. A network is comprised of *nodes*, or individual people, who are linked to each other by *edges*, or connections. Using these building blocks, Simler invokes several more concepts from epidemiology:[23]

23.   Kevin Simler, "Going Critical," *Melting Asphalt*, May 13, 2019, https://meltingasphalt.com/interactive/going-critical/.

- *Transmission rate*: The probability that an infected node (person) will successfully spread an idea to its edges (connections)
- *Immunity*: The percentage of nodes in a network that are categorically resistant to infection

Put simply, when an idea tries to spread from one person to another, it's not guaranteed that that person will be equally enamored by the idea (expressed as *transmission rate*), in the same way that having the flu doesn't guarantee that you will spread it to every person you interact with. And some people will be completely resistant to the idea whatsoever (expressed as *immunity*).

If immunity is sufficiently low, and/or transmission rate is sufficiently high – as was more common in the Web 2.0 era – an idea is considered memetic, meaning that "infected" nodes are eager to spread the idea to others, who likewise tend to be receptive to that idea. Cute cat videos, for example, were more viral in 2010 than they are today, when fewer people were immune to this type of content.

While not *all* content that's difficult to spread is antimemetic, being highly resistant to spread is a key property of antimemes. Antimemes have not just a viral coefficient, but a drag coefficient as well: the amount of resistance that must be overcome before the idea can spread more easily. Some antimemes reach escape velocity and become memetic, while others remain obscure yet stable, and still others are deliberately suppressed and eventually die out.

Immunity and transmission rate are determined not just by the qualities of the idea itself – how innately viral it is – but how receptive its nodes (that's us) are. The same idea might be memetic within certain networks, but antimemetic in others. Flat earth theory, for example, spreads easily through a small but strong network of enthusiasts, while most other networks seem to resist infection. Some "extremely online" social networks might be deeply preoccupied with the latest gaffe on Twitter, while other networks have no idea what Twitter even is.

Changing the properties of the idea – such as the format or structure it's presented in – can influence a network's transmission rate and immunity, but these properties are always subjectively defined by what resonates with the network. Emphasizing the aesthetic benefits of regular exercise, for example, will resonate better with young, attractive 20-somethings who don't know what arthritis is, whereas the health benefits are a bigger draw for 40-somethings who are feeling the early pains of middle age. Even though the core concept is roughly the same in both circumstances, changing how it's messaged can help it spread more easily through different networks.

Finally, we can add a third variable to our study of how ideas spread: the *symptomatic period* – or how long an infected node actively "expresses" the idea. Symptomatic periods measure an idea's *impact*, or how consequential it is to the network. Just as getting the common cold is very different from getting cancer, some ideas pass quickly, while others grip us for much longer.

Memes typically have short symptomatic periods. Consider how long it takes for you to read a funny post on social media, for example, and text it to a friend. Unless it's especially good, you'll probably forget about it within minutes.

Antimemes, on the other hand, tend to have much longer symptomatic periods. Antimemes are *hugely* consequential; they can derail not just our lives, but the communities we belong to, which is why we suppress them. As a result, we nodes tend to have strong built-in immunity to antimemes, so that we don't harm our networks by introducing a big, disruptive idea without good reason.

With these three properties of *immunity, transmission rate*, and *symptomatic period*, we can now examine how antimemetic ideas become memetic. While ideas sometimes appear to come out of nowhere, they can often result from subtle shifts in the dynamics of a network.

AS CANCEL CULTURE WHIPPED itself into a frothy peak in late 2016, its vortex claimed the body of one rather obscure and nerdy software engineer, who appeared to be otherwise indistinguishable from all the other casualties. His name was Curtis Yarvin; he had been working on an indecipherable piece of software called Urbit for more than 15 years; and he was no longer allowed to give a talk at the upcoming LambdaConf – a conference for software developers – because news of his upcoming appearance had caused an alarming number of speakers and sponsors to drop out.

From 2007 to 2014, Yarvin had written a blog, called *Unqualified Reservations*, under a pen name, Mencius Moldbug, in which he argued that modern liberal democracy had failed to deliver on its promises. Instead, Yarvin believed that we ought to revert to hierarchical forms of government, such as monarchy or corporate-style leadership, which prioritize order, stability, and centralized control.

The first line of *Unqualified Reservations* reads: "The other day I was tinkering around in my garage and I decided to build a new ideology."[24] In this endeavor, Yarvin had succeeded. Along with the writings of philosopher Nick Land, Yarvin's blog formed one of the canonical texts underpinning what came to be known as the neoreactionary movement (often abbreviated to NRx), or the Dark Enlightenment. While *Unqualified Reservations* had a niche audience, its premise – challenging the prevailing belief that liberal democracy was the most desirable form of government – introduced a new paradigm to the political discourse.

---

24. Mencius Moldbug, "A formalist manifesto," *Unqualified Reservations*, April 24, 2007, https://www.unqualified-reservations.org/2007/04/formalist-manifesto-originally-posted/.

At the time of Yarvin's cancellation, NRx was usually mentioned with a smirk, if it was ever mentioned at all. The term was used as shorthand for a bunch of weird internet philosophers LARPing about overhauling our democratic institutions and bringing back the kings. But with time, the Dark Enlightenment came to inform the resurgence of what's now called the New Right, a contemporary strain of conservative political thought that's characterized by a deep skepticism of globalism, an emphasis on national sovereignty and local community values, and a results-oriented approach to governance. Once seen as a fringe movement, the New Right gained wider recognition after it was covered by journalist James Pogue in *Vanity Fair* in 2022. These ideas reached the national stage when Donald Trump named JD Vance – who, though not a monarchist, spoke favorably about Yarvin's views on cutting through bureaucracy and dismantling the "administrative state" – as his running mate in their successful 2024 bid for the United States presidency. Regardless of what you might think about Yarvin's views, the trajectory of his ideas, from random blog to U.S. presidency, presents a powerful case study on how antimemes can make their way into public discourse.

Back in 2016, not everyone who disapproved of Yarvin was concerned with his views on democracy and monarchy. In fact, many people were unaware of his core thesis at all. (Not that they could be blamed; Yarvin's writing style is notoriously circuitous, making it difficult to untangle what he is really trying to say.) Instead, the condemnation of Yarvin stemmed from a much more salient transgression: a few lines in *Unqualified Reservations* where he expressed his views on race and intelligence, which were not good or admirable, are not endorsed by this author, and do not bear repeating here.

Yarvin's dismissal as a LambdaConf speaker seemed to be the nail in his career's coffin. Yarvin was done for, and his name was not to be mentioned in polite society, lest his tarnished reputation taint the speaker's as well. From a network perspective, transmission rates plummeted to an all-time low.

But Yarvin's cancellation had a bit of a Streisand effect. Public condemnation of his views made more people rush, albeit privately, to read what he had said that was so bad. And it just so happened that the (non-race-related) views he expressed on *Unqualified Reservations* found fresh relevance as a working explanation for the tumult and chaos that people faced in 2016, in the wake of a U.S. presidential election that rocked the country and the world. Though it wasn't obvious at the time, Yarvin wasn't yet finished. Instead, he was just embarking upon a journey from scapegoat to martyr.

I had been unaware of Yarvin's existence, nor the controversy surrounding his reputation, when a friend recruited me to co-present a conference talk about governance in 2018. The conference was hosted by a company called Tlon, which stewarded the development of Urbit. I had no idea what Urbit was, either, and trying to read about it just confused me even more. But I liked my friend, and I liked the topic, so I agreed to present the talk. At the last minute, she pulled out, but as a conciliatory gesture, swapped in a different friend to collaborate on the talk with me.

Crammed into a booth with our laptops at Four Barrel Coffee in the Mission neighborhood of San Francisco, my new partner – whom I was only lightly acquainted with at the time – shot me a mischievous glance.

"So...you know there are people who wouldn't approve of going to this conference, right?"

"What do you mean?" I asked.

Twenty minutes later, I had gotten the full download on Urbit, Yarvin, and the Dark Enlightenment. From what I'd gathered, Yarvin was the founder of Urbit, and he had been kicked off a conference speaker lineup due to controversial remarks he'd made on his blog many years before. But it wasn't until I arrived at the conference that I finally understood what Urbit – and by extension, Yarvin himself – represented to its followers.

The first thing I noticed was that the crowd was not what I'd expected. I had been to a lot of software conferences at that point, and the attendees here were...different. Less uniformly technical, less aesthetically predictable. It looked more like a cultural movement than a professional gathering. We were not at a convention center or in an oppressively lit conference room, with people in brightly-colored T-shirts and lanyard badges shouting over the din. We were in a stylish, wood-framed glass house nestled among sandy Californian dunes, and the murmurs were calm and peaceful. As I mingled with the group, I spoke to a monk, then a lawyer, about how they had discovered Urbit and resonated with its ideals. Then the programming began, and I finally got to hear about the vision from the Urbit team itself.

Urbit's CEO – a former architect – kicked off the event at the podium with his opening remarks, in which he cited the 1965 essay, "A City is Not a Tree," by architect Christopher Alexander. "Why is it that so many designers have conceived of cities as trees," he asked, "when the underlying structure is a lattice?" Social networks, he thought, were not meant to be single networks – centralized, highly public platforms like Facebook, Twitter, and Instagram – but a centerless network of networks, which would preserve each community's culture and context.

Afterwards, Yarvin took the stage. "Every city is its own social graph," he declared. There would never be another single social graph like Facebook. What society needed was a restoration of trust, and "we can't have a high-trust society that's also a war zone."

Yarvin's speech was the first time I'd heard someone not just argue for divestment from our social platforms, but actually present a vision for what an online social graph could look like instead. Back then, his position seemed avant-garde and vaguely transgressive. Today, it could have been uttered by any one of us. His words reverberate in the comments of Hannah Sung, the journalist who wrote about group chats' benefits in a *New York Times* op-ed: they are "a refuge where my ideas and thoughts don't have to be fully formed and battle ready."

Urbit is not Yarvin; nor is it his blog, *Unqualified Reservations*. At the nadir of his cancellation, Yarvin was so concerned about protecting Urbit, his beloved brainchild, from his own tarnished reputation that he resigned from the project in 2019. But it is impossible to separate creative projects from the visions of their architects. What drove Yarvin to create Urbit contains echoes of that which drove him to write *Unqualified Reservations*. They came from the same mind, around the same time, and put forth a similar vision for the world: to give everyone their own patch of the universe where they could be who they wanted to be, undisturbed by hostile outsiders.

To the extent that software is both art and an ideology, Urbit was a full-stack expression of what a compartmentalized world would look like if every group chat became a fortress or a mafia. Yarvin – who founded Urbit in 2002 – tried to build a small-scale diorama of this world, well before all the messaging apps and newsletter platforms and decentralized social media protocols that followed.

Standing in that room at the Urbit conference and watching the waves crash against the shore, it became clear to me why, in the tumultuous wake of the 2016 U.S. presidential election, so many people had rediscovered Yarvin's work and found something meaningful in it. At a time when no one was allowed to breathe a word about it in public – online or offline – Yarvin offered a simple, compelling explanation as to why the world was going topsy-turvy: our social platforms had become too public, and the only solution was a return to smaller, high-context spaces.

While Yarvin is best known for his philosophical contributions to the New Right, I think that's the least interesting part of his work, even if it was materially consequential. Yarvin was the first prominent figure, at least among my circles, to foresee the inevitable transition from highly public online spaces to more private ones.

When I returned to San Francisco from the conference, I started looking for others to talk to about Yarvin's ideas. It turned out that a *lot* of people I knew were reading his work – and, like me, not mentioning it unless asked. In epidemiological terms, many of the nodes in my network were "infected," but the transmission rate was still low. What had previously gone unseen in my social interactions suddenly became visible to me, the newly initiated. And the lack of visibility, of course, only made his ideas more interesting. Yarvin was officially an antimeme.

There was no predictable way that a connection in my network would bring up Yarvin's name in conversation. It was usually in the context of a trusted interaction, where we'd gone back and forth enough around related ideas, that someone would then feel comfortable enough to mention his work. If you could tolerate Yarvin, you were "marked safe" as a person one could say, "What the *heck* is happening right now?!" to, without having to explain what that meant, nor risk being cancelled yourself.

Yarvin's ideas benefitted from long symptomatic periods that enabled them to survive, even though they couldn't spread. Eventually, it no longer felt like lone, one-off individuals, but small groups of people who were comfortable openly discussing his work, so long as they knew who they were talking to. Dense networks – software engineers, certain circles in tech, Dimes Square and the Red Scare fan community – privately incubated his ideas until they reached critical mass years later.

Yet Yarvin remained invisible on the public web. For a time, I felt that I was operating in a liminal space where many of the smaller groups I spent time in and around knew who Yarvin was and what his ideas were (though they often had conflicting views on his merits), yet no one would dare speak his name in public. From a game theoretical perspective, they weren't yet confident that enough *other* people knew about Yarvin that there wouldn't be negative consequences to openly mentioning his work. Most of their connections still appeared to be *immune*, or resistant, to infection, and it was hard to know who had flipped without risking one's personal reputation.

I'm not sure when I realized that at some point, it was no longer transgressive to mention Yarvin's work. There was no single "aha" moment, though I noted a growing frequency with which new, and often unexpected, acquaintances would bring him up in early conversation. As nodes began to infect other nodes, Yarvin simply faded into view, slowly and imperceptibly, until his presence became self-evident, and I could no longer remember a time where it wasn't. By the time Yarvin appeared on *Tucker Carlson Today* in the fall of 2021, his crossover to the mainstream discourse affirmed what the rest of us already knew: that after half a decade of cancellation, Yarvin was acceptable to recognize in public again.

TABOOS ARE ONE OF the most prominent categories of antimemes, and they make for good case studies on the mechanics of network *immunity, transmission rates,* and *symptomatic periods*. Some taboos – such as stealing, cheating, or lying – don't budge within most networks. Immunity to the idea is too high, or transmission rates too low. But taboos linger precisely because their symptomatic period is so long. They can lie dormant for years until more nodes are willing to receive or spread the idea, at which point taboos become volatile and unstable, pushing their way towards the light.

After years of lingering in the shadows, Yarvin-as-taboo managed to reach escape velocity once immunity began to decrease (the culture wars intensified, leading more people to search for explanatory frameworks), and transmission rates improved (people began to cautiously, then actively, spread Yarvin's ideas until there were enough "infected," though siloed, networks to support Yarvin's emergence onto the main stage).

Antimemetic ideas often grow within dense, high-context networks. Multiple networks might incubate the same forbidden idea simultaneously, but because they're disconnected, ideas can't "jump the gap" between them. Despite being perfectly visible within a smaller network, the object remains invisible, or antimemetic, to the collective whole.

During this incubation period, networks don't necessarily know what other networks are thinking, or if others are even aware of these same ideas at all. They operate in silos until there is a "big reveal" – a test of public sentiment, where disparate groups reveal their positions simultaneously in hopes of gaining favor. How much a network chooses to reveal, however, depends on incomplete information about other networks' positions.

In a memetically charged environment, it's safer to frame ideas as independent, uncoordinated opinions rather than as part of an organized movement – closer to a mafia, or guerrilla-style information warfare, than a public advocacy group. This tactic makes it harder for opposing forces to single out and target who is really behind an idea, which enables it to spread more organically.

To illustrate how this works, imagine a group chat called the Monday Mafia, whose members share a controversial belief that isn't widely accepted: "Mondays should be outlawed." Mentioning this idea in public settings would get them fired, cancelled, or worse.

The general public is unaware that the Monday Mafia exists, nor who its members are. Although there are dozens of members in this group, no one discloses their affiliation in public, because keeping it secret enables them to express their views more credibly, avoiding accusations of collusion.

Finally, a news item pops up. Someone did a study, and it turns out that people are more likely to be depressed on Mondays than any other day of the week. The Monday Mafia spots an opportunity to make a bid for destroying the reputation of Mondays in public. But rather than announcing themselves as a united public front – as political interest groups or unions might have historically done – just one member, Groucho Garfield, publishes a social media post, in which he laments how awful Mondays are. To the public, Garfield only represents himself.

Someone from the Monday Mafia drops a link to Garfield's post in the chat. "Great job, Garfield!" Other members of the Monday Mafia share Garfield's post on public channels, then publish their own statements in support of his position. Similarly, they all appear to represent only themselves, with no mention of their group affiliation. It now appears that many unaffiliated people – not just Garfield – believe that Mondays are awful and should be outlawed. This creates the illusion of broad, uncoordinated agreement, which lowers the social cost for others to join the anti-Monday movement.

Most anti-Monday supporters will never realize that the Monday Mafia exists, but members occasionally add more people to their group if they think someone is a particularly outstanding contributor. Similarly, inactive members are also regularly culled from the group to maintain a high-trust environment.

This strategy – presenting as individuals in public, while keeping group membership private – helps ideas spread in a Dark Forest landscape where the public is highly sensitive, and often hostile to, the tribes they don't belong to. Trying to make the tribe appear bigger and more threatening would only put a target on its back; it's more effective to weaponize individualism.

Just like group chat membership itself, these tactics are self-censoring. It is nearly impossible to publicly document the existence of these effects without losing one's private member standing. Here is writer Tiago Forte, tweeting about the concept – with, of course, no specific example given:[25]

> *The key to Twitter is joining an informal cabal of mutually retweeting people with aligned agendas. Then you all interact with each other as a kind of performance art. But you can't ask or apply formally. It's all implicit, like collusion around price fixing.*

These public signaling games become more interesting – and risky – with subsequent battles for the same idea. For any one skirmish, colluding to amplify an idea is not that risky for the Monday Mafia. The public doesn't know who belongs to the group, so its members only stand to benefit from endorsing each others' views. With repeated iterations, however, if members are too obvious in their mutual support, people might figure out they are part of the same group, which reduces the effectiveness of their signaling. In order to maintain their influence over public discourse, members must carefully balance how frequently and overtly they support each others' views to avoid being "outed."

If the Monday Mafia is publicly identified, all is not necessarily lost, but the game advances to the next stage. Other, siloed networks with similar views – say, the Weekend Warriors or Weekday Abolitionists, who *also* secretly despise Mondays – might come out in support, forming a bigger anti-Monday coalition that snowballs into a powerful memetic force. What once seemed taboo suddenly appears to achieve widespread acceptance. The idea "goes critical" – to borrow Simler's phrase – by reaching a tipping point where its spread accelerates rapidly – not

---

25. Tiago Forte (@fortelabs), "The key to Twitter is joining an informal cabal of mutually retweeting people with aligned agendas. Then you all interact with each other as a kind of performance art. But you can't ask or apply formally. It's all implicit, like collusion around price fixing.," Twitter (now X), June 13, 2019, https://x.com/fortelabs/status/1139234130682699777.

because the idea itself has changed, but because network immunity has weakened, and transmission rates have surged.

However, if other networks fail to rally, or it turns out there are fewer like-minded groups than previously believed, the Monday Mafia risks being cast out by the public, who dismisses them as a "fringe" interest group. The Monday Mafia might recruit a fresh crop of members to conceal their affiliations, then try their hand at a skirmish again. The game resets and plays again.

FROM THE COZY HAUNCHES OF HINDSIGHT, we like to mock the reluctance of prior, unenlightened versions of ourselves – or our ancestors – to accept what were once taboos. But I think the slow acceptance of taboos is a feature, not a bug – even for taboos that eventually came to be seen as morally good.

People resist spreading taboos throughout their networks because of how consequential they are. Whether these consequences are good or bad, taboos are, by definition, cognitively expensive to assimilate. Nodes are instinctively protective of their networks, and they recognize the threat that antimemes present, which makes them reluctant to spread such ideas.

Qntm, the TINAD author, captures these fears skillfully in his fictional universe. His protagonist, Marion Wheeler, watches a past version of herself warn her urgently about the dangers of interacting with antimemes:[26]

> *[W]hen you make "eye contact", it kills you. It kills you and it kills anybody who thinks like you. Physical distance doesn't matter, it's about mental proximity. Anybody with the same ideas, anybody in the same head space. It kills your collaborators, your whole research team. It kills your parents; it kills your children....*

26. Qntm, *There Is No Antimemetics Division* (self-pub., 2021), 48.

> *Do you see? It's a defense mechanism. This information-swallowing behavior is just the outer layer, the poison coating. It protects the entity from discovery while it infests our reality.*
>
> *And as years pass, the manifestations will continue, growing denser and knitting together... until the whole world is drowning in them, and everybody will be screaming "Why did nobody realize what was happening?" And nobody will answer, because everybody who realized was killed, by this system...*
>
> *Do you see it, Marion? See it now.*

Though it might have challenging implications, resisting new ideas is an essential safety mechanism that's part of any cohesive network. Even morally good taboos – universal voting and property ownership rights, freedom of speech, desegregation – could take down a network and cause unintended harm if introduced too quickly. The abolition of slavery in the United States, for example, while obviously a moral good, also radically transformed the Southern states' agricultural economies, which relied heavily on slave labor for the production of cotton and tobacco.

Introducing a controversial idea carefully does not mean that it is any less valuable. On the contrary, it underscores its importance. Such ideas are so valuable that they must be handled delicately to ensure their survival. As we saw with the Monday Mafia example, a naive bid for public favor without support from smaller networks will be swiftly snuffed out. Networks need to be inoculated to avoid triggering an immune response.

I think of networks as a sediment filter for assimilating taboos. Sediment filters use mechanical filtration to make water cleaner, trapping suspended matter – dirt, sand, clay – as water passes through. Similarly, ideas need to be filtered through a network's nodes before they are ready for wide distribution. If the sediment filter is too porous, radical ideas plop into our laps too quickly, before people are ready to grapple with their implications, and we destabilize the network. On the other hand, if the sediment filter is *too* dense, radical ideas take too long to make their way into mainstream thinking, and we get stagnation. Determining the optimal filtration rate is more art than science.

Even Yarvin, at the height of popularity, was subjected to the network's sediment filter. While some of his ideas gained widespread acceptance, others have not, and are (in this author's view) unlikely to. It may no longer be controversial to agree with Yarvin that public social platforms fell short of globalists' promises of peace and democracy, and that this might warrant rewriting our social infrastructure. But many people still stopped short of bandwagoning onto the New Right's political agenda, or – even more extremely – a return to monarchy. And certainly for Yarvin himself, being welcomed back to society did not include welcoming his views on race and intelligence that first got him cancelled, which are still firmly sanctioned.

Taboos have no moral valence. They are not innately naughty or bad, and conversely, taboos that become widely accepted are not necessarily "good" or "right." A society that allows its longstanding taboo on racism to erupt into genocide is *mechanistically* indistinguishable from a society that allows its longstanding concerns about the ethics of slavery to erupt into a concerted push towards abolition – in the same way that truths and falsehoods can both spread memetically through the same distribution channels.

Ideas follow the same path from obscurity to acceptance, regardless of their moral implications. Because every taboo – regardless of its content – is an existential threat to the network, we must be careful about what we permit to enter its bloodstream. The rejection rate of taboos is high, but the payoff for patience is that when they do stick, their influence can be strong and enduring.

MEMETIC
GALAPAGOS

3

LET'S RETURN TO QNTM'S FICTIONAL UNIVERSE, where antimemes are imagined as monsters that swallow our minds. TINAD's heroine, Marion Wheeler, is sitting in an airlocked, bulletproof isolation chamber, watching a video recording of her former self.[27]

> *"You've guessed already that SCP-3125 is not in this room," she says. "In fact, this is the only room in the world where SCP-3125 is not present. It's called 'inverted containment'. SCP-3125 pervades all of reality except for volumes which have been specifically shielded from its influence. This is it. This is our only safe harbor."*

In the memetic city, group chats – along with other types of secluded online interactions – are our version of inverted containment chambers, which we built to shield ourselves from social media's memetic contagions. *Out there* was where the crazy stuff went down: people screaming at each other over the slightest perceived transgressions, shilling the Current Thing, scrolling dumbly for hours through the comments of a single, inconsequential viral video. *In here*, we were safe: surrounded by trusted friends and colleagues who shared our views of the world, where we could finally discuss controversial topics with nuance.

This, it turns out, was the equivalent of saying: "I don't want to get COVID, so I'm only going to socialize with ten of my most trusted friends." Theoretically, and even in practice, this could work – *if* your ten trusted friends also avoid getting infected with COVID. But if even one person breaks the pact by interacting with the outside world, and brings the virus back to the group, your "pod" sanctuary is going to look a lot more like a superspreader.

Political activist Eli Pariser warned about the harms of what he called "filter bubbles" in his 2011 book of the

27. Ibid., 47.

same name, in which curated news feeds and social circles lead us to believe our reality is the only one that exists. Back then, filter bubbles were still painted in the wash of Obama-era techno-optimism, where exposure to ideas was considered the lifeblood of democracy. Pariser and his peers worried that if people weren't exposed to conflicting or divergent opinions, they'd become stubbornly attached to their views.

Pariser's version of filter bubbles looked something like COVID pods, or what we imagine group chats to be, where each group is perfectly segmented from the other, with no new ideas ever introduced. Depending on one's goals, this level of isolation can be desirable (in the case of COVID pods) or not (in the case of filter bubbles).

Dense, isolated networks *appear* to be more stable and harmless, but they have weak immune systems. High trust between nodes means that they are more receptive to ideas – *any* ideas – that are introduced to the group, which can infect its members at an alarming rate.

COVID pods don't work in practice because realistically, you can't expect all ten of your friends to never interact with anyone else. Similarly, joining a group chat doesn't mean you are completely cut off from outside contagions. If anything, you are probably part of many different group chats, and therefore perfectly capable of cross-pollinating ideas that are being incubated in highly concentrated environments. It is like spending one's days moving between several poorly-ventilated rooms, instead of walking around all day in fresh air. By confining ourselves to close quarters, we accidentally created the ideal conditions for idea-viruses to grow – and mutate.

Isolated environments lead to greater speciation and biodiversity, a concept famously discovered by Charles Darwin during his studies of the Galapagos Islands. Darwin noticed that if two island species descended from a common ancestor, they would evolve different traits based on their microenvironment. Finches, for example, had different beak shapes, depending on the type of food available on their particular island. Since there's limited exposure to genes from outside populations, new species continue to evolve in strange ways, without dilution from external influences.

Group chats are like social islands. As fast as the internet's public highways might be, ideas evolve even *more* rapidly in private online environments. Ideas are tested, iterated upon, and refined, with little outside influence to temper the process, as they adapt to the unique dynamics of their members – much like Darwin's finches.

Just as the Galapagos Islands gave Darwin a laboratory to observe natural selection in action, group chats offer a way for us to observe how ideas evolve in the context of dense networks. In his "Going Critical" essay, Kevin Simler attempts to model some of these dynamics in a simulation. One of his simulations depicts a few small, tightly clustered nodes (the "urban" environment), embedded in a larger, looser network (the "rural" environment).

If the transmission rate is sufficiently high, an idea will take over both urban and rural areas. If it's too low, it doesn't take over either. But if it's somewhere in between, it takes over the urban networks, but not the rural ones. As Simler points out, whether these dense and loose networks represent urban versus rural settings, high school students versus their parents, elite versus non-elite networks, or – in our case – the private versus public web, the point is that dense networks are more susceptible to infection than loose ones:[28]

> *We tend to think that if something's a good idea, it will eventually reach everyone, and if something's a bad idea, it will fizzle out. And while that's certainly true at the extremes, in between are a bunch of ideas and practices that can only go viral in certain networks.*

28. Ibid.

Simulation of an idea-virus that starts in a looser network...

Simler, "Going Critical."

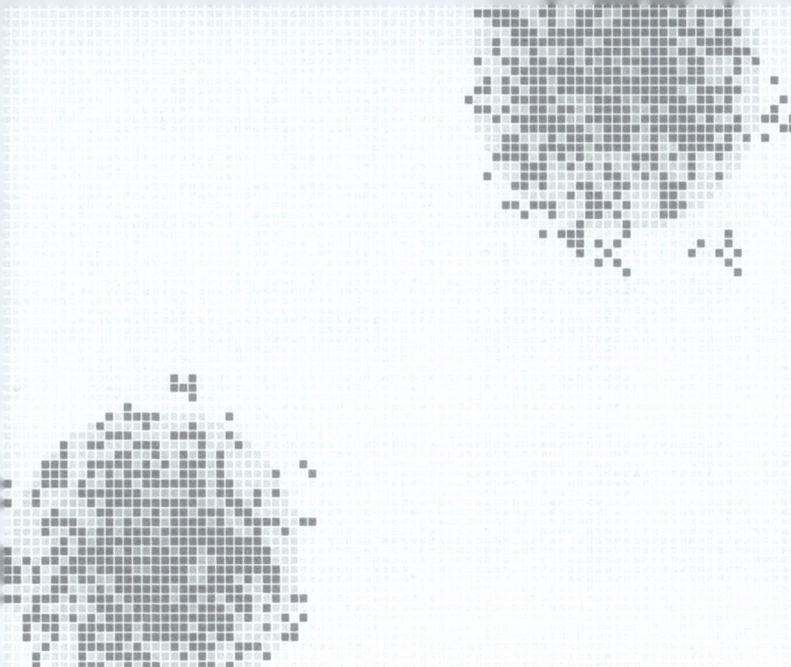

...then spreads and stabilizes, leaving only the denser networks infected.

Simler, "Going Critical."

Most people's group chats are benign – like Sophie Haigney's group chat, "The Girls." Its members are either immune to memetic contagion – we might call this being "very offline" – or transmission rates are low. (Picture, if you will, that one friend with crazy uncle energy who's always dropping memes and links in the chat. Their friends might find them entertaining, but don't take their ideas seriously.)

But for group chats where nodes *are* more susceptible to infection (to be "extremely online" is exactly as it sounds – one who is regularly exposed, and receptive, to lots of idea-viruses), *and* transmission rates are high, bringing everyone closer together has only made contagion worse – like Erik Prince's group chat, "Off-Leash." Group chats offer a false sense of protection from the chaos of the public web. They are an even denser, and therefore more transmissible, version of the internet.

As we've seen with all the antimemetic phenomena we've explored thus far, there is historical precedent for these behaviors. Dense, offline networks – such as small towns – exhibit similarly "safe," yet vulnerable, qualities. Before mass media communications like radio, television, and the internet, small towns were intellectually cut off from the world, which meant they didn't capture all the upside of progress, but also avoided its downsides.

Sometimes, however, a small town would get spontaneously infected by an idea, which exposed their weak immunity as the idea spread rapidly through the network. The Salem witch trials, for example, were sparked by whispers that spiraled into hysteria. Its residents' lack of experience with confronting unusual ideas enabled paranoia to grow unchecked, which led to wild and unforeseen outcomes.

One theory as to why cults flourished in the 1960s and 1970s might be due not just to the politically charged environment of the time – more of a symptom than a cause – but the new ways in which ideas were able to spread. The United States interstate highway system was built in the late

1950s, under President Eisenhower, just as the color television first arrived in households across America. Small towns were suddenly hit by a deluge of ideas from new forms of transportation and mass media, but they lacked the ability to process these ideas effectively. Just as the ideas from public social platforms spread and mutate among group chats today, small American towns became fertile ground for extreme ideologies to take root.

IN OCTOBER OF 2020, the FBI revealed they had arrested thirteen men as suspects in a plot to kidnap Michigan governor Gretchen Whitmer. The idea began in a paramilitary group called the Wolverine Watchmen: a dense network of like-minded extremists who met and coordinated via Facebook Groups and in encrypted group chats. Several members were active on YouTube, where they posted videos expressing their frustrations with Whitmer's handling of the COVID-19 pandemic.

Private online spaces enabled these members to meet, and amplify their influence, in ways that wouldn't have been possible otherwise. Without these spaces, they might have remained isolated, passively consuming content on platforms like YouTube or Facebook from others who shared their extreme views, but never forming actual relationships. Offline, they likely would have kept their views private to avoid social or legal consequences.

With group chats and private online communities, however, members' grievances were not just validated, but allowed to evolve into more extreme beliefs. The plot to kidnap Whitmer began at an in-person meeting organized by members in Ohio. A discussion about creating a new, independent society quickly turned to frustrations over the pandemic and perceived government overreach in mandating lockdowns. What might have otherwise remained as private anger escalated into a call to violent action, as the Wolverine Watchmen developed an elaborate kidnapping plot that included a "kill house," field training exercises, and surveillance of Whitmer's vacation home.

The upside of cults, utopian societies, and other social islands in the pre-internet "memetic Galapagos" is that, because they were physically and socially isolated, their ideologies rarely spread far. After infecting the entire network, ideas had nowhere else to go, and would ultimately fizzle and die – sometimes literally – with their members. While many cults committed violent crimes during their active days, in the long run, the extreme ideas that drove them to do such things were of little enduring social consequence, save as unusual footnotes in the history books.

In the context of private online spaces, however, members are still exposed to other networks, whether they are scrolling on their favorite social media platforms or participating in other group chats. Not only are they more likely to bring new contagions into the group, but they are also more likely to spread their group's idea-viruses to other networks. A highly infectious idea that might have once died within the confines of a lone, fringe network can now jump between groups, enabling it to live on indefinitely.

If we plot the *transmissibility* of an idea against its *impact,* or how consequential is, we can discern a more fine-grained taxonomy of the types of ideas that move through networks:

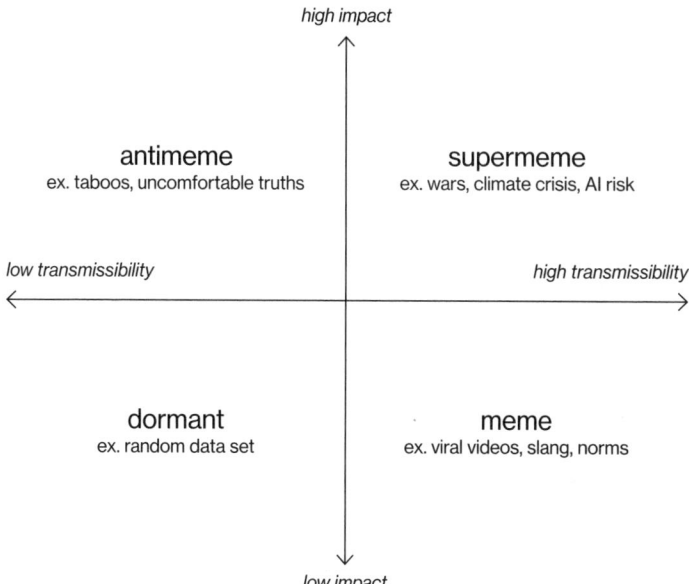

Antimemetics – Why Some Ideas Resist Spreading

Type	Description	Example
Supermeme	The "black hole" of memes. Supermemes spread easily and infect people for a long time. Their impact generates a strong gravitational pull that sucks in everything around it.	Wars, cultural movements, revolutions; some social causes, like population decline or the climate crisis
Antimeme	Highly consequential ideas that face strong resistance from the nodes in a network. Like fiber, they move slowly through the system and take time to digest.	Taboos; life lessons and lived wisdom; uncomfortable truths
Meme	Highly transmissible, but their impact is low. Like sugar, these ideas are consumed voraciously, but pass through our system quickly. We don't engage deeply with their underlying premise.	Viral videos and images; slang; norms, rituals and traditions
Dormant (non-memetic)	A general catch-all for "noise." These objects don't spread easily and are of little consequence, so people filter them out to focus on other, more important things.	Random data set; complex legal documents

Now, rather than just memes and antimemes, we can classify cultural objects – ideas, people, items – as being *memetic, antimemetic, supermemetic,* or *dormant (non-memetic)*.

Your average garden-variety meme is highly transmissible, but largely inconsequential. Memes die out quickly, or else pass through us unconsciously. Cultural norms like handshakes or saying "bless you" when someone sneezes are memetic, but we don't think much about them. Even more consequential memetic behaviors, like marriage or working a salaried office job, don't require much energy to process, because most of us were socialized into these norms and don't question their underlying premises. The meme itself doesn't consume much of our attention.

Supermemes, on the other hand, are like black holes. Like memes, they spread quickly, but unlike memes, they are perceived as *highly* consequential. Their sheer gravitational force pulls us in, crowding out our ability to think about anything else. Whereas antimemes are characterized by a "strange forgetting" by the perceiver, supermemes are characterized by a "strange inability to forget." If antimemes provoke avoidant behavior, supermemes are closer to being trapped in a rumination loop.

Why do supermemes grip our minds, while antimemes are ignored or forgotten? Supermemes combine multiple *attractors* – ideas that exert a natural pull on our attention – into a single, digestible idea, which creates a magnetic pull. Attractors often resonate with our deepest fundamental values, fears, or aspirations, which make them impossible to resist. Supermemes typically contain the following characteristics:

- *An appeal to strongly-held values:* Fears about overpopulation or population decline, for example, are charged because they appeal to our beliefs about family, morality, and social responsibility.
- *Perceived widespread impact:* Existential risks, such as from biological threats or artificial intelligence,

theoretically affect everyone on Earth, which makes them feel urgent to address.
- *Lack of specificity*: There is a surprising lack of consensus, for example, as to what the "climate crisis" actually means, nor how to measure its progress.

In short, supermemes frequently take the form of a civilizational threat that demands us to prioritize it over everything else. In the vein of "No one ever got fired for buying IBM," doomsday scenarios are easy to justify working on, because "No one can blame me for wanting to save the world from destruction." And, just as how armies spring up to rally around a common cause during wartime, supermemes give rise to talent ecosystems that help them spread and survive for longer periods of time.

Until recently, supermemes were relatively rare. War is human civilization's oldest supermeme: as Girard might put it, a violent outgrowth of mimetic competition for limited resources. It forces everyone in the network to direct their attention towards a single narrative. Compulsory drafts ensure that everyone and their families, regardless of social class, give up everything – including their lives – to war. War has a sweeping impact on economies, careers, and cultures. Historically in the United States, its effects were visible in everything from the GI Bill, which funded World War II veterans' college tuition and democratized higher education, to the Harlem Renaissance, as African-Americans migrated north from the rural South to fill urban labor shortages during World War I.

Today, war is no longer a defining cultural narrative for most of the Western world. Although war certainly hasn't disappeared on a global level, and Western militaries are still active abroad, it is not something that civilians living in Western societies have a personal stake in anymore. Instead, they conscript themselves into the service of other supermemes, some of which exist in parallel. In recent decades, these have included:

- *Climate change* and its associated crises, such as peak oil
- *Existential risk* associated with artificial intelligence
- *War on religion* and Christian values
- *Overpopulation* (in the 21st century) and *population decline*
- *Fear of foreign threats*, such as the Soviet Union (during the Cold War), China, or Islamism

Just as isolated environments in the Galapagos allowed species to adapt and specialize, the private web – with its many dense networks – fostered the emergence of diverse supermemes. What was once a single, unifying supermeme has now "speciated" into many rare and exotic forms, each uniquely tailored to the needs and values of its network.

How did we evolve from just one supermeme to a veritable open market? Keen observers will notice that the supermemes listed above all appeared after World War II. They are often grouped under the umbrella of "culture wars": a fairly new concept in American history, despite the extent to which it embroils all of us who dare to peek at the news today.

The Cold War – with its blend of McCarthyism and proxy wars in Korea, Vietnam, and Cuba – represents a sort of hybrid transition period between the epochs of world wars and culture wars. During the Cold War, Americans were gripped by the ideological and military struggle between the United States and the Soviet Union. The presence of an external, foreign threat created a unifying purpose: destroying communism and asserting Western dominance on a global stage.

With the collapse of the Soviet Union in 1991, however, the United States found itself without a clear external adversary. In the absence of a unifying conflict, Americans broke new battleground with the "culture wars" – a term popularized around the same time – where they could fight over issues related to identity, morality, and values.

From an outside perspective, war is about fighting for limited global resources like power, physical territory, and cultural hegemony. But domestically, it also offers a salve for mimetic desire and competition, as it gives citizens a common place to direct their attention – towards an external threat. Patriotism (and its more extreme counterparts, nationalism and jingoism) is a unifying force; a fear of outsiders brings people together quickly.

Without a foreign threat to distract us from within-group differences, however, civilians become restless and start picking fights with each other. Their attention turns to angling for new territory: control over their social institutions.

Social institutions – whether media, academia, or the political machine – are the bottlenecks through which all ideological demands must eventually pass. To truly change culture, one must master control of these institutions. But the Digital Age created a flood of new ideas that are all competing for roughly the same, limited set of physical resources. Government budgets can only be allocated to so many places; Congress can only vote on so many new bills per year; Harvard can only accept so many students per year; *The New York Times* can only publish so many new articles at a time. Culture wars intensify when too many competing ideas are jostling for limited paths to change, which is why improving the speed and efficiency of institutional response becomes critically important during "(culture) wartime."

While we can identify a few, distinct waves of culture wars – say, the religious fights between neoconservatives and New Atheists in the early 2000s, versus the wokes and anti-wokes of the late 2010s and early 2020s – it would not be far-fetched to say that we've been embroiled in a prolonged and escalating mimetic conflict since the end of the Cold War. Girard believes that mimetic conflict is resolved by scapegoats, but as we've seen, they don't help unify a fragmented landscape of disparate communities, because one man's scapegoat is another's martyr.

A temporary reprieve from the culture wars came after the September 11, 2001 terrorist attacks, as Americans were briefly united by a renewed focus on foreign threats. The national motto became "United We Stand," and public attention shifted to wars abroad in Afghanistan and Iraq. But this unity was short-lived as the motives behind these wars were contested, and the idea of unity itself was repurposed as fuel for the next wave of culture wars. Debates over topics like patriotism, national security, and government overreach became battlegrounds that divided Americans along ideological lines, reigniting internal conflicts that – it turns out – had only been temporarily suppressed.

If global wars are a grab for physical land and resources, culture wars are a grab for mindshare. Our slow migration from broadcast media channels, to social media platforms, to group chats can be seen as an ongoing effort to expand the frontiers of human attention and thereby relieve us from the zero-sum competition for mindshare. But every progressively smaller fiefdom still needs a *raison d'etre*. There has never been a perfectly peaceful community in the history of mankind: people always need conflict – no matter how trivial – to give them purpose and strengthen ties. (Ask anyone who lives on a college campus or retirement community how the most trivial gossip can take on mammoth proportions. Who brought whom back to their room last night? Who forgot to bring brownies to book club?)

Supermemes bid ruthlessly for our attention. In doing so, they often take on a dark and apocalyptic tone. This sets them apart from other social issues, such as global poverty or animal rights, which don't have these qualities, although some supermemes also started out more innocuously. Environmentalism is one case study that demonstrates how ideas can transform from mere "social cause" in the early 20th century to a supermeme today.

Prior to the Cold War, environmentalism was seen more as a distinct movement that one might opt into, rather than an all-encompassing force. In the early 20th century, "caring about the environment" was narrowly defined as the stewardship of natural resources, which grew into two related, yet distinct schools of thought – *conservationists* (such as Teddy Roosevelt and Gifford Pinchot), who wanted humans to use nature responsibly; and *preservationists* (such as John Muir), who wanted to leave nature untouched – that reigned for at least half a century. The establishment of the National Park Service in 1916, along with organizations like the Sierra Club, National Geographic Society, and National Audubon Society, reflected the formalization of these early movements.

By the 1960s, however – that strange transition period between global wars and culture wars – environmentalism took on a more alarmist tone, with conservationists questioning the effects of a post-WWII society that was newly enamored with mass production. In 1962, the biologist Rachel Carson published her manifesto *Silent Spring*, which stoked public fears about the harmful effects of pesticides and kicked off a new, advocacy-oriented "Greenpeace generation" of environmentalism that was primarily concerned with the harmful effects of human consumption and economic growth. As public concerns grew, U.S. Senator Gaylord Nelson fought to establish the first Earth Day in 1970 in order to direct more attention onto environmental issues. His, and others', efforts were a success: the Environmental Protection Agency (EPA) was created under President Richard Nixon later that same year.

The activist era of environmentalism continued for several more decades, becoming more anti-corporate- than regulation-focused over time, including more extreme branches of so-called "radical" environmentalism, such as ecoterrorist organization Earth Liberation Front (ELF), which frequently used arson in its tactics. Finally, the late 1990s marked a third era of environmentalism that converged on a shared apocalyptic scenario, called "global warming" – bringing us to today.

Even in this new, post-Cold War version of environmentalism, however, climate didn't become a supermeme until much more recently. From roughly the 1960s through the early 2000s, "being an environmentalist" was a distinct identity that most people did not affiliate with. It was certainly not considered to be part of one's day job, outside of activists and nonprofit workers.

Climate became a supermeme in the late 2010s. There was a clear change in public opinion towards climate change around this time. Yale University's Program on Climate Change Communications (YPCCC), which has tracked public attitudes towards climate change for more than a decade, shows that their most concerned category ("Alarmed") grew sharply starting in 2018, nearly doubling from 18% in 2017 to 33% of American adults surveyed in 2021.[29] It was no longer enough to merely protect the environment anymore; we had to save civilization from extinguishing into a fireball.

There are specific events that probably contributed to this cultural shift, including a 2018 IPCC special report that described the impacts of 1.5°C global warming to the public, and the publication of *The Uninhabitable Earth: Life After Warming*, a book by David Wallace-Wells in 2019 that might be described as a modern *Silent Spring*. But the acceleration of the climate crisis may have also been driven by changes in how we communicate. The late 2010s overlaps with the rise of social media, which may have caused certain supermemes – like the climate crisis – to make the leap from niche social cause to urgent, doomsday

---

29. "Global Warming's Six Americas," Yale Program on Climate Change Communication, accessed December 20, 2024, https://climatecommunication.yale.edu/about/projects/global-warmings-six-americas/.

scenario. The term "doomer" became popular starting in 2018, thanks to a popular 4chan meme.

The climate crisis also splintered into memetic tribes during this time, each with its own beliefs and agenda. The Breakthrough Institute, for example, with its focus on eco-modernism and technology-driven solutions, has little in common with Extinction Rebellion, which advocates for radical, disruptive action through civil disobedience to halt environmental destruction. As these tribes retreated to the private web, there was no single version of a "climate advocate" anymore. Instead, climate tribes had evolved into a variety of exotic "species," each adapted to the conditions of its community.

In the global war era, Westerners only dealt with one supermeme at a time. In the Dark Forest era, many supermemes can flourish concurrently, supported by an archipelago of dense networks. Private online spaces created the ideal conditions for these supermemes to grow. Find enough people who share your views, no matter how extreme or far-fetched, and they will form your new reality.

I AM OF TWO MINDS about how we should interact with supermemes. The first is a warning. Supermemes are like a dangerous, antibiotic-resistant mutant strain of meme that we haven't yet developed widespread immunity to. They demand our attention – *all* of our attention – like a shadow that appears in the corner of your eye. Its mere presence demands that we look at it, keeps us from feeling fully absorbed in other pursuits. There's a prickly sensation at the back of our necks that leaves us wondering: what the heck is that thing doing over there, and shouldn't I figure out what it is?

When supermemes lack a clear focus on specific outcomes, they can trap people in a state of permacrisis that never fully escalates or resolves. A supermeme without practical application will loop upon itself indefinitely, as we dissect its virtues with likeminded people in group chats, conferences, and on our public feeds – citing statistics and imagined futures – without ever putting these ideas into practice. The only way to break the cycle is to shift the conversation from ideas to action.

Supermemes, perhaps perceiving that the physical world can "call their bluff," strive to preserve themselves for as long as possible by marshaling as large of a talent network as they can. It is the supermeme equivalent of the "industrial complex" phenomenon that plagues bureaucracies, where an idea ceases to have attainable goals and instead tries to perpetuate itself for the sake of living on.

Supermemes are like an invasive species. When too many supermemes crowd a network, they can threaten its comparatively more diverse and generative creative ecosystem. Simler uses the example of academic research to demonstrate how this works in "Going Critical." He distinguishes between Real Science, or "whatever habits and practices reliably produce knowledge," and careerists, who are "motivated by personal ambition." Careerists "gum up the works" of Real Science communities, promoting themselves instead of contributing to the growth of shared knowledge. As Simler puts it, careerism "may look and act like science, but it *doesn't* produce reliable knowledge."

And so it is with supermemes. They may look and act like interesting ideas, but they are primarily selfish, doing whatever it takes to prolong their existence. Supermemes are like catnip for hordes of creative and knowledge workers – technologists, academics, artists, activists. But they are intellectual sinkholes, vacuuming up every resource they can acquire, and when they take over a network, there is little attention left to focus on anything else.

Fixating on the next big crisis is a recipe for perpetual distraction. To protect our attention, then, we must learn to resist the temptation of supermemes. For those who haven't developed strong immunity, the best cure is prevention: staying far away from ideas that look like supermemes.

...On the other hand. We are here to examine the shape of ideas as they are, not as we wish they could be. In a crowded universe of narratives, the reality might be that ideas need to shout more loudly to be heard. Perhaps supermemes are a useful format to cut through the noise and spur people to action. From a zoomed out perspective, this means that instead of directing everyone's attention to a single world war, or going to the moon, or defeating the Russians, society can now support many different "critical missions" simultaneously. Maybe civilization isn't distracted, after all; it's just scaling up, and we now have an increased capacity to tackle more problems at once.

Crises can be an effective way to spur ideas to action. Operation Warp Speed was a remarkable example of rapid coordination between the private and public sector to develop and manufacture a COVID-19 vaccine during the pandemic. Researchers, government officials, and private companies came together in May 2020 to develop vaccines that might've otherwise taken years to create. By that December, just months after the initiative began, the first vaccines were approved for emergency use. Perhaps most notably, Pfizer and BioNTech developed a vaccine using relatively new and unproven mRNA technology, backed by billions in government support. Its success opened the door for a new wave of research into other mRNA applications beyond the pandemic's needs, including vaccines to treat other infectious diseases like HIV and influenza, cancer treatments, and personalized medicine.

Operation Warp Speed showed how all-consuming ideas can drive meaningful action when resources, talent, and willpower are aligned. It helped that the people involved in Operation Warp Speed were working towards a specific outcome, which – combined with the urgency of the pandemic – forced them to move out of the ideas world more quickly. It also meant there was a clear end to the operation after it had served its purpose. Not every supermeme has this quality, but the presence of a productive goal might help us discern which supermemes are worth letting ourselves get sucked into. (Simply having a goal isn't necessarily enough: I'm thinking of the flurry of DAOs and NFT communities in the 2022 crypto boom that had specific goals, but perhaps not productive ones, which led many people to act in risky and irresponsible ways that they otherwise wouldn't have.)

Instead of avoiding supermemes, then, perhaps it's that we just need to be careful about which ones deserve our attention. Supermemes have no intrinsic value except as an organizing tactic: as heartwrenching or alarming as they might be, we cannot let ourselves be swayed so easily. If we pledge our attention to every supermeme that comes our way, we will lose ourselves in the process.

Nodes, again, have a critical role to play here as gatekeepers: they can help prevent a supermemetic outbreak from taking over the entire network. Cancel culture illustrates how networks can develop such immunity. At first, every public "cancellation" was treated equally, because people hadn't developed an intuition for which transgressions were worth paying attention to. As the cancellations mounted, however, it became clear that one could not spend every day reviewing all the terrible things that every human has ever done – there are not enough hours in the day – so eventually, people stopped spreading every story and became more discerning.

Every person has their own decision tree for evaluating which transgressions to take seriously; it is not my intent to evaluate what that framework should be. The point is that there has been a clear evolution from the mid-2010s – where people were more receptive to every new "cancellation" news story – to the mid-2020s, where some nodes are now immune or resistant to spread, while others have varying rates of transmission. It takes time, but with sustained, repeated exposure, networks adapt to manage memetic overload.

Just as war can be a senseless outbreak of violence and destruction, some supermemes are equally senseless. But the tornados they whip up can be quite powerful. Supermemes can help us accomplish more big civilizational goals in parallel – so long as we're careful about which ideas we feed into the wind machine, and which we allow to sweep us off our feet.

THUS FAR, WE'VE PRIMARILY EXPLORED how ideas spread through networks at a bird's eye level. Networks, at this altitude, look like a depersonalized constellation of nodes. But nodes are just people – they're *us*! While ideas do have intrinsic qualities that influence their spread, it's also clear that we, as individuals, play an essential role in determining whether ideas flow through, or die with, us. It's a big responsibility, especially when evaluating taboos or supermemes, where stakes are high for the network.

In the next chapter, we'll zoom in to the atomic level and examine how we, as nodes, decide to pass new ideas onto our connections. Attention is the key mechanism that governs this process: it shapes not just our personal realities, but our collective behavior. Focus your attention on something, and it sharpens and becomes omnipresent. Let your attention wander, and the object blurs and fades away.

WE ARE OUR ATTENTION

4

We Are Our Attention

IN THE LAST FEW DECADES, there's been a new wave of what's called "advanced meditation" that offers access to deep, intense mental states – from the euphoric, to psychedelic, to voluntary loss of consciousness – all of which are achieved solely through sustained concentration.

One type of advanced meditation unlocks a series of altered states referred to as the *jhanas*. Practitioners experience strong versions of highly positive emotions, ranging from buzzy thrills to a pervasive sense of peaceful "okayness" – much like a "panic attack for joy."[30] This isn't your average mindfulness meditation app.

For many people in the West, meditation is synonymous with mindfulness practices that emphasize open awareness. In this approach, meditators are encouraged to stay present with whatever arises – sounds, thoughts, sensations – without focusing too much on any one thing. The goal is to cultivate a sense of calm and nonreactivity, where a person can perceive all things as part of a larger experience without feeling moved to respond.

But this is only one version of what is possible with meditation. Less commonly practiced is a style where, instead of keeping awareness wide and open, a person trains their attention on a specific object – such as the breath, a phrase, or a positive feeling. As the mind zeroes in, remarkable things can happen. Distractions fall away, a sense of self fades, and perception of time dissolves as a person enters a heightened state of effortless concentration.

If you've ever been in flow state – lost in a great conversation, toiling on a creative project, deeply absorbed in your workout – you know exactly how this feels. This style of meditation just makes it possible to invoke flow states *without* the use of external stimuli. Instead of having to strap on your skis and carve the hills to get that sweet feeling of

---

30. Oshan Jarow, "What if you could have a panic attack, but for joy?," *Vox*, June 7, 2024, https://www.vox.com/future-perfect/354069/what-if-you-could-have-a-panic-attack-but-for-joy.

perfect synchronicity with the universe, with enough practice, you can conjure it in your body at any moment.

A highly focused mind, in a state of flow, amplifies whatever it's given. If you train it on writing code, you'll code effortlessly for hours. If you train it on an anxious thought, you'll spiral into a panic attack. And – it turns out – if you train it on joy, you'll burst into a radiant euphoric state known as the first jhana.

Most casual meditators never encounter these states, simply because this style of practice isn't as widely known or discussed. Most popular meditation schools in the West, such as Vipassana, don't teach the jhanas. Some teachers view them as distractions from insight, cautioning against attachment to the pleasurable bodily sensations associated with the jhanas. Many also believe that meditators need years of practice to enter these deep mental states.

In recent years, a handful of teachers in the West revived the jhanas. New teaching methods made them easier to access in shorter amounts of time: sometimes days or weeks, instead of years. As more people – including Bay Area technologists – discovered the jhanas, they took to Twitter to tell others what they'd experienced.

Intrigued by the chatter on my feed, I pitched a magazine about writing a piece on the topic. As part of my research, I signed up for a retreat myself. I had virtually no meditation experience, save for a Zen retreat I'd attended with a friend over a decade before.

With the guidance of my retreat instructors, I found myself in first jhana – intensely euphoric, comparable to taking MDMA – in less than an hour. Over the next four days, I progressed through nearly all the jhanic states, each with its own distinct and surreal qualities. In fifth jhana, my mind floated out of my body to gaze at an infinite space. In sixth jhana, it exploded with indescribable, psychedelic beauty that – in seventh jhana – dissolved into nothingness.

The jhanas offer a rare glimpse into the extent to which our minds construct the world around us. As someone who had hardly ever meditated before, what surprised me most was not just the actual sensations, but realizing that such extraordinary states had been locked away in my mind this whole time. Their existence demonstrates that attention, when summoned to its full strength, can pull off some incredible and counterintuitive feats.

Attention is how we carve our personal realities: it is the breathing valve of our consciousness. *Selective attention*, or the act of focusing on one object at the expense of others, determines what we perceive. Like a flashlight, selective attention illuminates whatever it is aimed at, while other, equally "real" objects fade into the shadows. As I type in a café right now, I am able to write because I'm unconsciously filtering out the café's music, the murmur of other patrons, and the clatter of baristas preparing coffee.

This skill – which some meditators hone to an extreme – are a marvelous bit of wizardry that comes pre-installed in our brains. Using only our minds, we can make the world as beautiful or ugly as we wish.

SELECTIVE ATTENTION IS AN ESSENTIAL SURVIVAL SKILL, but it also creates blind spots – hidden cognitive biases that dictate what we do or don't see. The same mechanism that allows us to summon flow states can also filter out ideas that are inconvenient or mentally demanding. These blind spots are a type of antimeme that all of us experience regularly.

Economist Robin Hanson and Kevin Simler – who authored the "Going Critical" essay discussed previously – explain how attention shapes conscious experience in their book, *The Elephant in the Brain*. Our brains gently steer us towards narratives that make us feel good, and away from those that don't. When someone donates a large sum of money to a charity, for example, they tend to frame it as selfless altruism, rather than acknowledging motives like gaining power or assuaging guilt. These hidden, selfish motives are antimemetic: they remain invisible to the perceiver, because noticing them would present a challenge to how they see themselves.

Hanson and Simler emphasize that this behavior is universal, and having such base desires doesn't make you a bad person. They even reflect honestly on their reasons for writing their own book, acknowledging motives like a desire for status and prestige. Yet even they – the authors of a book dedicated to uncomfortable truths – admit they were "relieved for the chance to look away" after finishing their book. As they observe, "It's just really hard to look long and intently at our selfish motives."

We avoid thoughts that are cognitively expensive to process. But ignoring these ideas doesn't make them go away. Our antimemetic motives loom large in our minds: the eponymous "elephant in the brain," silently guiding our choices.

Hanson and Simler use the term *self-discretion* to describe how our brains suppress highly consequential information. When we encounter an idea that disrupts our current version of reality, our brain "conspires – whispers – to keep such information from becoming too prominent." As we saw in Chapter 2 with the spread of taboos, we do this not just to protect ourselves, but to avoid passing potentially damaging information onto others, including those we love or want to impress. "Feel the pang of shame? That's your brain telling you not to dwell on that particular information. Flinch away, hide from it, pretend it's not there. Punish those neural pathways, so the information stays as discreet as possible."[31]

The Elephant in the Brain is about one type of antimeme: selfish motives that threaten our self-image and social standing. But this same energy-preserving mecha-

---

31. Robin Hanson and Kevin Simler, *The Elephant in the Brain: Hidden Motives in Everyday Life* (Oxford University Press, 2018), 88-89.

nism filters out *any* antimemetic idea or task that demands significant mental effort to process. For example, I am reminded of a particularly pesky to-do list item that I put off, week after week, after my son was born: sitting down with my husband to write our will.

This task was an antimemetic albatross – seen and forgotten once a week – that I shuffled dutifully across my calendar. I knew it was important to write a contingency plan in case the worst happened. Though the scenario was unlikely, the consequences of neglecting it could be serious for the people I love. Nonetheless, estate planning is annoying work for two people with busy lives. Every week, I'd see it on my to-do list and bump it to the next week.

No one wants to think about their own death, much less the death of themselves and their partner simultaneously, and the horrible implications it would carry for those left behind. (This seems like a good time to quote Hanson and Simler, who lamented that discussing their book was "a real buzzkill at dinner parties."[32]) Death, retirement planning, getting married and having kids…for many people, these ideas are difficult to prioritize because they force us to confront uncomfortable truths. Hanson and Simler note how ideas that emphasize altruism or cooperation spread easily: "By working together, we can achieve great things!" These ideas are memetic because they're inspiring and easy to share. By contrast, ideas that emphasize competition or harsh realities often "suck the energy out of the room" and struggle to spread.[33]

From this perspective, antimemes are an immune response to cognitive overload. Whereas memes only require a small fraction of our attention and are cognitively cheap to engage with, antimemes are highly consequential and are cognitively expensive to grapple with. To protect our attention and avoid disrupting our daily lives, our

32. Ibid., 13.
33. Ibid.

"unseeing" defense mechanism kicks in, and the object slips by undetected.

Any major change in our circumstances, especially those that tie to psychological and spiritual needs, frequently presents as antimemetic. It is difficult to occupy two opposing realities simultaneously, which can also make it difficult to empathize with prior versions of ourselves – and, by extension, anyone who reminds us of who we once were.

When you're happy, you forget what it was like to be unhappy. When you're in a fulfilling relationship, you forget what it was like to be single. When you're financially comfortable, you forget what it was like not to have money. When you have close friendships, you forget what it was like to be lonely. When you're healthy, you forget what it was like to be physically impaired.

This type of antimeme poses a challenge for medical professionals who prescribe treatments for ailments that must be followed long after symptoms have subsided – such as antibiotics or physical therapy – or mental illnesses, such as antidepressants, anti-anxiety medication, and antipsychotics. When these treatments work well, patients feel good and have difficulty recalling how they felt before – so they stop. One study by The Pew Health Group found that even though most participants knew that the "correct" answer to taking antibiotics was to complete their prescribed course of treatment, nearly everyone in the focus group "admitted they failed to do so, often stopping in mid-course when they began to feel better."[34]

Handwashing, too, suffers from antimemetic headwinds. Despite a strong public social norm towards handwashing, and clear scientific evidence demonstrating its

---

34. Hart Research Associates and Public Opinion Strategies, "Americans' Knowledge Of And Attitudes Toward Antibiotic Resistance: A report of findings from a national survey and two focus groups," The Pew Health Group, November 2012, https://www.pewtrusts.org/~/media/legacy/uploadedfiles/phg/content_level_pages/in_the_news/abxpollsummarypdf.pdf.

value, compliance is absurdly low, even in medical settings. According to one meta-analysis, the mean handwashing compliance rate in the intensive care units (ICUs) of high-income countries – in other words, the type of place we'd expect compliance to be highest – is only 64.5%.[35] It's not that people don't understand the importance of taking antibiotics or washing their hands; they just can't seem to stay engaged with these practices. Our health and wellbeing is an all-consuming goal when we don't have it – but, once obtained, strangely fades from our conscious thoughts.

Attention is a precious, limited resource. We can't expect to fully engage with every idea that enters our headspace. Yet at the same time, it's clear that relying too heavily on unconscious filters can leave us blinded to opportunities that would otherwise be useful to "see."

Given that tradeoffs are inevitable, I find myself wishing for *some* sort of moral framework with which to evaluate whether I'm investing my attention wisely. Is it equally "good" to focus on human rights activism, versus spending time with my family, versus scrolling on Twitter all day? What is our imperative regarding where to allocate our attention – if there is one at all?

IN HER SHORT STORY, "The Ones Who Walk Away from Omelas," Ursula Le Guin describes a town called Omelas that stands shining by the sea. The gardens are covered with moss and the roads are lined with trees. Children play in the streets; there is no suffering or conflict. But this idyllic setting conceals a disturbing, antimemetic secret: the residents' happiness depends upon the imprisonment of one child, who is kept in misery and confinement. Everyone in Omelas knows about the child, and the horrific conditions it must endure, but they do not do anything about it,

---

35. Kathryn Ann Lambe et al., "Hand Hygiene Compliance in the ICU: A Systematic Review," *Critical Care Medicine* 47, no. 9 (2019): 1251-1257, https://doi.org/10.1097/CCM.0000000000003868.

because doing so would require sacrificing their own happiness.

One way to interpret Le Guin's story is as a parable about moral complicity. The child in the story represents the oppressed and exploited members of society upon whom our comfort and happiness depends. We are asked to expand our attention to take in all the unseen realities we've filtered out of sight, and to consider whether we would continue to live in Omelas with the knowledge of the bargain required, or be one of the few who walk away.

In attempting to apply this lesson to the real world, however, I am overwhelmed by the number of tradeoffs I face in my daily life. How easy it would be if there were only *one* child from Omelas held captive in the basement of our consciousness, instead of hundreds or thousands! Global poverty, human trafficking, worker conditions in warehouses and factories, factory farming of animals...an entire shadow city of suffering lies behind every basic task in our modern world today. And in the age of supermemes, where we are navigating not just one Really Big Narrative but an entire marketplace of them, we are exposed to even more of these moral dilemmas today, with each one screaming that they are the most urgent and consequential one.

Refusing to engage with difficult ideas – even those that point towards the deep suffering of our fellow humans – does not necessarily make us cruel and callous, or even selfish. No one can expect to fully address, and reconcile, every dilemma they face. When our attention is being pulled in infinite directions, deciding where to direct it isn't a simple moral question of "good" versus "bad," but a practical question of how to spend our limited resources. We need to decide *which* uncomfortable truths to prioritize and which to let go.

We could try to resolve the dilemma of infinite choice by treating it as a problem of utility maximization. This is the view promoted by utilitarianism, which emphasizes acting in ways that maximize happiness and minimize suffering for the greatest number of people. Implied is that there is some discoverable way to rank the relative importance of issues and allocate our attention accordingly, using metrics like "lives saved" or "quality-adjusted life years."

Effective altruism is a philanthropic movement inspired by utilitarianism, and it uses evidence and reason to determine the most effective ways to help others. Effective altruists prioritize actions that maximize positive impact, and in some cases, have developed elaborate algorithms to define what "positive impact" actually means.

But such calculations always reflect the values of those who create them. What one person deems most important – whether it's alleviating global poverty or combating climate change – is shaped by personal, cultural, and historical contexts. Even metrics that seem purely quantitative mask subjective choices about what we value most. Focusing on causes that prioritize improving lives abroad versus those in our local communities, for example – or vice versa – is a matter of personal values.

Le Guin's story is a testament to the importance of intuition and taste, which prevents us from accepting utilitarianism as a wholesale solution to the problem of prioritization. Omelas is a dark version of the utilitarian world in which happiness is technically maximized for the most number of people (the rest of the town), but comes at great cost (the child). Her story resonates because – for most people, anyway – it just doesn't feel right to outsource our judgment to a game of numbers.

In his book *Strategic Giving: The Art and Science of Philanthropy*, philanthropy scholar Peter Frumkin identifies a key consideration for developing philanthropic strategies, which he calls instrumental versus expressive giving. *Instrumental giving* focuses on measurable outcomes and is driven by a desire to solve specific, often large-scale social problems with efficiency and precision – like the effective altruists' approach. *Expressive giving*, by contrast, emphasizes the personal values, beliefs, and identity of the donor.

Impact is measured according to individual or community values, even if the outcomes are less deterministic.

Frumkin's telling of history suggests that we've already seen the utilitarian worldview play out. With the passage of time and rise of professional norms in philanthropy – accelerated especially by restrictions imposed by the 1969 Tax Reform Act, such as stricter reporting requirements and mandatory payouts – Frumkin argues that philanthropy went too far in the direction of instrumental giving. An overfocus on efficiency turned into a race to the bottom, where all philanthropic strategies became indistinguishable from one another.

Philanthropy is meant to be pluralistic, reflecting a diverse expression of values from private citizens who exercise the freedom to put their money wherever their ideas are. Instrumentalized philanthropy, on the other hand, starts to mirror the role of government, where there is a single, authoritative way of doing things. Philanthropy and government should ideally work in tandem, where experiments funded with private funds can derisk and inform what's eventually adopted at the institutional level with public funds. But if philanthropy is too prescriptive, it stifles the experimentation it is supposed to enable.

We can use these two philanthropic dimensions – instrumental versus expressive – to inform how to allocate our attention in a way that benefits our networks. The utilitarian approach feels like monoculture farming. If everyone uses the same calculation to determine where to allocate their attention, we will create a brittle system where too many people do the same type of work, which reduces overall fitness and leaves us vulnerable to blind spots.

Instead of trying to engineer a perfect hierarchy of attention, we should aim to cultivate a "biodiverse" information ecosystem that thrives on a multitude of interests pursued by each of its members. In biology, ecosystems with greater biodiversity are more resilient to shocks and better equipped to adapt to changing conditions. Similarly, a healthy network benefits from having many different nodes pursuing what each finds most meaningful or compelling. Not every gatekeeper will uncover a transformative idea, but the sheer diversity of approaches increases the likelihood that someone will. A decentralized network of curious minds makes the information ecosystem stronger, more adaptive, and more likely to produce ideas that take off.

Each of us, then, is left to decide how we want to prioritize our attention, according to our own values and interests. But how should we balance our personal interests with those of our networks? Is what's good for us, as individuals, always good for the group?

"OUR ATTENTION IS BORN FREE, but is, increasingly, everywhere in chains," declared a trio of activists in a *New York Times* op-ed.[36] Graham Burnett, Alyssa Loh, and Peter Schmidt are members of the Friends of Attention collective, a network of "collaborators, colleagues, and *actual friends*" that formed in 2018 due to shared concerns that our attention is being hijacked for others' private gain.[37]

Friends of Attention organizes lectures, educational workshops, and performative art to remind the public that there is a war being waged on our attention, and that we need to fight back and reclaim control. They compare the fragmentation of our attention to fracking, or the practice of cracking the Earth's bedrock to extract oil and natural gas. Profiteers, they claim, are "pumping vast quantities of high-pressure media content into our faces to force up a spume of the vaporous and intimate stuff called attention, which now trades on the open market. Increasingly power-

---

36. D. Graham Burnett, Alyssa Loh and Peter Schmidt, "Powerful Forces Are Fracking Our Attention. We Can Fight Back.," *The New York Times*, November 24, 2023, https://www.nytimes.com/2023/11/24/opinion/attention-economy-education.html.

37. "About the Friends of Attention," Friends of Attention, accessed December 20, 2024, https://www.friendsofattention.net/about.

ful systems seek to ensure that our attention is never truly ours."

I first encountered attention activism when I read Jenny Odell's book, *How to Do Nothing*, less than a year before the COVID-19 pandemic began. Odell, an artist and activist based in Oakland, California, frames "doing nothing" as an act of political resistance to what's often called the *attention economy*, or the buying and selling of attention in a market, like that between advertisers and media properties."[38] Advertisers compete for sellers' attention like casinos bidding for the most degenerate gamblers, tracking consumers' eyeballs and sentiments and using this information to place just the right ads in just the right places so that they can charge clients as much as possible. Widespread social media use ensures a steady stream of monetizable attention. The producers of attention – that is, all of us – are treated as cattle in these transactions, shuffling around like zombies and staring with glazed eyes at whomever is the highest bidder.

Odell implores us to extricate ourselves from this system, pointing out – as I discovered on my meditation retreat – that where we direct our focus determines what becomes real. Mastering control of our attention is how we "not only remake the world but are ourselves remade."[39] Odell is fond of bird-watching, and she recounts how spending her time on the study of birds and local ecology, rather than on her phone, transformed her perception of the world:[40]

> *More and more actors appeared in my reality: after birds, there were trees, then different kinds of trees, then the bugs that lived in them....these had all been here before, yet they had been invisible to me in*

---

38. Jenny Odell, *How to Do Nothing: Resisting the Attention Economy* (Melville House, 2020), xi.
39. Ibid., 94.
40. Ibid., 122-123.

previous renderings of my reality.... A towhee will never simply be "a bird" to me again, even if I wanted it to be.

I share the activists' views that taking a hard look at our attention, and how it is being spent, is an important step in helping people reclaim a sense of agency over the world. Researchers Robert Emmons and Michael McCollough once showed that when students were asked to keep a daily journal about what they were grateful for, as opposed to recording their grievances, they reported significantly more positive moods – as well as prosocial behavior, such as helping others with personal problems or offering emotional support.[41] People who are unhappy or dissatisfied with their lives – irrespective of their circumstances – would almost certainly benefit from directing their attention to what brings them joy, which also makes them more likely to make positive contributions to their communities.

Where we direct our attention also shapes more than just our personal realities: it influences which ideas do or don't spread through our networks. The same critique of utilitarianism – that it leads to idea monocultures – applies to unregulated attention economies. Networks ultimately rely on their nodes to evaluate new ideas. If we let others hijack our ability to engage with difficult or complex ideas, we risk shirking our duties as gatekeepers. Giving away our attention to the loudest, flashiest voices in the room ultimately creates a world where we're all parroting the same set of banal ideas.

Nevertheless, I find myself somewhat dissatisfied with the solutions offered by the attention activists, who tell us to "remain in place" as a means of reclaiming our attention, but in a way that seems disconnected from our

---

41. Robert A. Emmons and Michael E. McCullough, "Counting Blessings Versus Burdens: An Experimental Investigation of Gratitude and Subjective Well-Being in Daily Life," *Journal of Personality and Social Psychology* 84, no. 2 (2003): 377-389, https://greatergood.berkeley.edu/pdfs/GratitudePDFs/6Emmons-BlessingsBurdens.pdf.

responsibilities to the network. Odell, clearly exasperated by memetic overload, dreams of a world in which we free ourselves from "shouting into the void" on social platforms. Instead, she asks us to "replant [our attention] in the public, physical realm."[42] "Whether it's a real room or a group chat on Signal," she writes, "I want to see a restoration of context, a kind of context collection in the face of context collapse."[43] Her words reflect a widely felt, contemporary desire to escape the memetic city's constant churn, seeking safety in smaller communities where we at least *know* who is vying for our attention, instead of letting it passively trickle out of our brains into the rushing rivers of our news feeds.

In a sense, Odell got what she wanted. Less than a year after *How to Do Nothing* was published, the COVID-19 pandemic broke out, and the world ground to a halt. Stay-at-home lockdowns forced us to re-engage with our local, offline worlds, even as it supercharged our online ones. We baked sourdough bread as we scrolled our feeds, but – because we couldn't see our friends in-person as often, or as easily – we started spending time in smaller online contexts, too. We spun up group chats. We signed up for newsletters. We hosted book clubs and dance parties on Zoom. For a brief period, it seemed that the web had indeed benefited from a "restoration of context." As a popular meme of the time proclaimed: "Nature is healing."

But the future that followed didn't quite look the way Odell envisioned, in which we "reinfus[ed] our attention and our communication with the intention that both deserve."[44] The reemergence of the private online web was not a mere reversion to Web 1.0, where people socialized on blogs, email chains, and internet forums, blissfully disconnected from a shared narrative. Instead, the web is now composed

---

42. Odell, *How to Do Nothing: Resisting the Attention Economy*, xi.
43. Ibid., 176.
44. Ibid.

of both public and private spaces, and these two worlds are closely intertwined.

Odell imagines that in a space that is "small and concentrated enough...the plurality of its actors is un-collapsed."[45] But, like a genie wish gone awry, the rise of Signal group chats didn't necessarily lead to a nuanced landscape of ideas so much as a balkanization: a memetic Galapagos where dense networks lead to even greater and weirder idea speciation, which then make their way back into public contexts, both online and offline. While some group chats are innocuous – the kind that Odell had hoped for – a global restoration of context also made our world darker and stranger and more unrecognizable than before.

When confronted with the noise and unpredictability of the public web, it can feel good to retreat to quieter spaces, whether that's the private web or our local communities. If our attention is truly ours to spend as we wish, there should be nothing wrong with this behavior. But retreating from the chaos only protects ourselves. It is akin to fleeing to gated communities or the suburbs to avoid the dangers of cities, burying ourselves in the comforts of "local community," while avoiding the hard work of getting things done at civilizational scale. Taken to its logical conclusion, the divestment of all members from public spaces destroys the integrity of those spaces.

Odell, for her part, recognizes this concern and explicitly cautions against escapism. In a chapter titled "The Impossibility of Retreat," she warns us from following in the steps of communes in the 1960s or seasteading experiments in the late 2000s, reminding us that "there is no such thing as a clean break or a blank slate in this world," even as she acknowledges its temptations.[46]

It is hard to see, however, how one can fully embrace the invitation to "refuse" the world without becoming

45. Ibid.
46. Ibid., 53.

disengaged from solution building. Odell believes that periodically stepping away is a temporary, not permanent break from reality: a sort of mental reset that reminds us what our lives are really for. But this reminds me of the social media addicts who cycle through deleting and re-installing apps on their phone, instead of learning to cultivate a fluid sense of control in the world they've been given.

"Standing apart," in Odell's eyes, is "a commitment to live in permanent refusal," even when actively participating in public spaces.[47] But I find it exhausting to imagine standing in a permanently defiant position, hands on hips, feet apart. How can I learn to act decisively, from a place of ease and confidence, rather than bracing against a constant perceived tension?

Viewed through the eyes of the attention activists, I feel less like an empowered individual and more like a forever-branded piece of cattle that has been rescued from its captors: unchained, yes, but lacking purpose and direction. I don't just want to stand still; I don't want to be the naysayer in a sea of people who are doing and building things. There will always be a place for critics and whistleblowers, but if *everyone* did the same, the world would not be better in the long run. We can't hunker down indefinitely in cozyweb. Our public narratives and civilizational histories still need to be nurtured. We will always crave the wide, expansive feeling of awe – a supermeme to devote our lives to.

There is no wishing away the existence of the public online web. If we don't like what we see, we simply have to learn how to engage with it more deeply and meaningfully. We must pick up a paintbrush, find a blank canvas, and paint the world as we wish it to be. Instead of hiding in our safe and quiet communities, we need to summon the courage to step forward and attempt to do great things.

47. Ibid., 62.

IF ANTIMEMES ARE A DEFENSE MECHANISM in response to cognitive overload, we now know how to make things more or less antimemetic: by mastering control of our attention and wielding it to shine a light on whatever we want to make more real in the world. Whether we're filtering out distractions, grappling with moral dilemmas, or striving to create a better future, our attention is the tool that makes it all possible.

Attention is not something we merely *own*; it is what we *are*. Learning to wield it isn't just about returning to the "present moment," but rather about creating infinite, dazzling realities – because what we choose to see in the present moment is unique to each of us.

But reclaiming control of our attention isn't just about hiding out in cozyweb. Our attention is not meant to be commandeered by others, but it is also not ours to hoard. Even when it's hard, our responsibility to the network requires that we actively engage with, and contribute to, the world around us. There is no single answer as to which causes we ought to take up, and this is by design. When we pursue what each of us finds most interesting, we create a diverse ecosystem that benefits the network.

In the next two chapters, we'll apply everything we've examined so far – on the individual and network level – towards collectively advancing the causes we care about. I want to talk about us as magical wizards of attention, capable of waving a wand and transforming our worlds in astonishing ways. That seems a lot more fun to me than playing slots at the casino.

SACRED
KNOWLEDGE

5

Did you notice the giant box in this photo? If not, good.

Image source: Wikipedia, via user elisfkc2. Uploaded August 31, 2021, licensed under CC BY-SA 2.0. https://en.wikipedia.org/wiki/Go_Away_Green#/media/File:Ratatouille_(51414590388).jpg.

WHEN WE PICTURE A TRIP TO DISNEY WORLD, we might think about the majestic, colorful spires of the Cinderella Castle, or the big, golf ball-shaped structure that towers over Epcot. We probably don't think about the staff-only buildings, storage units, or electrical boxes and HVAC units, but Disney World's parks are rife with this sort of infrastructure, which supports some 120,000 visitors per day.

One of the reasons we don't notice these things is because Disney has coated them in an unremarkable shade of grayish green paint, nicknamed "Go Away Green." By painting these "undesirable" objects to match their surroundings, Disney directs our eyes to brighter, contrasting foreground objects. This technique works so well that we don't even process what is hiding right in front of us.

Antimemetic objects follow the same principle: they are often cleverly disguised against a foreground of memetic objects. Our minds snap to the visual "sugar" of a particularly outrageous or compelling idea, without noticing what isn't being said or seen. Just like Disney World's infrastructure, it's not that the plainer, quieter ideas are any less important – they're just better at staying out of sight.

Sometimes, we intentionally coat ideas in "antimemetic paint" to deter people from seeing them. Other times, ideas get mired in a sticky swamp of antimemetic mud that they can't seem to shake off, making them impossible to notice, even when we really should.

First off, for the free speech enthusiasts in the back of the room: why *wouldn't* we want certain ideas to spread? As we've seen in previous chapters, some ideas can cause chaos if the network isn't yet ready to receive them, so they can require caution – if not outright suppression – before we share them with our connections.

In his 2011 paper, "Information Hazards: A Typology of Potential Harms from Knowledge," philosopher Nick Bostrom explains how disseminating certain types of information, which he calls information hazards (or *infohazards*), can be harmful.[48] A few examples include:

- *Data hazards*, such as the genetic sequence of a lethal pathogen, a blueprint for thermonuclear weapons, or sensitive personal information, such as Social Security numbers or credit card information
- *Idea hazards*, such as the mere idea of using a fission reaction to create a bomb, assassinating a public figure, or introducing biological warfare
- *Signaling hazards*, which transmit unwanted information about the sender, such as their ignorance about a topic, sensitive political affiliations, or how they think

The policy prescription for infohazards is to suppress dissemination, which can be accomplished using either *hard* or *soft tactics*.

A hard tactic means the idea is explicitly forbidden to share, which is enforced by legal or social penalties. Hard tactics are used to keep sensitive data under tightly controlled settings. Corporations and governments suppress plenty of information this way, using legal contracts, such as a non-disclosure or non-disparagement agreement, or imposing heavy fees or even criminal penalties. Edward Snowden, the intelligence contractor who worked for the National Security Administration, leaked information about its global surveillance programs to the public. He was charged with espionage and had his United States passport revoked.

But hard tactics alone don't always succeed at memory-holing knowledge. Even if we can't directly access all the information that's forbidden to us, we can still know that it exists, and that it is being kept from us. Samo Burja

---

48. Nick Bostrom, "Information Hazards: A Typology of Potential Harms from Knowledge," *Review of Contemporary Philosophy*, vol. 10 (2011): 44-79, https://nickbostrom.com/information-hazards.pdf.

calls this type of proprietary information *intellectual dark matter*, or "Knowledge that we can show exists, but cannot directly access." Although corporate or government knowledge is not publicly accessible, we can infer it exists "because our institutions would fly apart if the knowledge we see were all there was."[49]

Paywalling information, then, doesn't necessarily make it antimemetic. If anything, it can make that information even *more* compelling to outsiders, as it acquires a mysterious, unattainable quality. A juicy secret that can't be shared can still spread memetically, even if its contents are never revealed. I am reminded of the "Eye Mouth Eye" prank that swept through tech Twitter in the summer of 2020, in which a small handful of people hyped up the following emoji: 👁—👁 for seemingly no reason. What started as a "shitpost" amassed into, in the span of a day, a 30,000 person "early access" waitlist, before its organizers revealed that there was nothing behind the curtain, and asked people to donate to a handful of social causes instead.[50]

While hard tactics can inadvertently draw attention to the thing they're trying to protect, soft tactics transform knowledge from bewitchingly *verboten* to boringly antimemetic. The HBO television show *Westworld* portrays a fictional adult theme park where humans interact with extremely lifelike robots, or "hosts," in a Wild West-themed setting. Human "guests" are invited to don a cowboy hat and live out their basest fantasies in a world with no real consequences. Because the hosts live and operate in the same environment as humans, they are programmed not to notice certain things that would cause any awareness or distress about their true nature. When they see something

---

49. Samo Burja, "Intellectual Dark Matter," *Samo Burja*, July 16, 2019, https://samoburja.com/intellectual-dark-matter/.

50. Arielle Pardes, "The 👁—👁 Debacle Sums Up Tech's Race Issues," *Wired*, June 29, 2020, https://www.wired.com/story/eye-mouth-eye/.

they shouldn't, such as sketches or diagrams of hosts, they calmly respond with, "It doesn't look like anything to me."

This sort of not-noticing is the antimemetic alternative to, say, *Men In Black*-style tactics, where a person's memory is aggressively wiped after they've noticed something they shouldn't have. The hosts on *Westworld* simply don't assign any deeper meaning to the things they see, despite their actual importance. Rather than being censored, it is seen and processed, but causes no distress. It is noticed, then ignored. It escapes detection, because it is perfectly antimemetic.

Social norms are one type of soft tactic that can gently dissuade the spread of undesirable information. You won't go to jail for telling everyone how much money you make, but it's generally understood – rightly or not – that discussing salaries with people you don't know well can make them uncomfortable. No one had to explicitly explain this rule to you; it's something you've (hopefully) learned by watching what others do and don't do.

Another soft tactic is to paint spicy ideas in Go Away Green: in other words, make them less interesting to others. Bostrom calls this tactic *obscurantism*, and it is a form of intellectual camouflage, just as animals in the wild use patterns and colors to blend into their surroundings and avoid predators. One can effectively divert eyes away from an idea by making it seem either totally repulsive or totally boring. A flashy mansion that's visible from the public street view will attract unwanted visitors, even with the best home security system or extremely tall hedge. Better to hide it from prying eyes, whether that's behind an unremarkable tangle of trees, or (as I've once seen) on the top floor of a parking garage.

Politicians are masters of this sort of spin. Alaska governor Sarah Palin coined the term "death panels" to refer to a provision in the Affordable Care Act (also known as "Obamacare") that would reimburse doctors for end-of-life counseling sessions with patients, which stoked public fear and resistance to the ACA. Palin made the ACA seem repulsive. On the other hand, "net neutrality" is an incredibly boring term for the notion of internet service providers (ISPs) treating all customers equally, regardless of willingness to pay – which likely played a part in its languishing and uncertain regulatory status in the United States.

Obscurantist writing is also called "Straussian" writing – named for the scholar Leo Strauss, who argued that throughout history, heterodox ideas were often cloaked in obscure, tedious rhetoric to avoid censorship and persecution. A thick coat of Straussian paint can help sensitive ideas travel across the public web, while also escaping detection. As Venkatesh Rao bluntly puts it:[51]

> *Any idiot can simply write posts in private cozyweb channels, encrypt posts and only share keys with trusted people, or use steganographic deceptions. The real trick is to write in intrinsically anti-memorable ways where despite the reader wanting to retain an idea they think is important, they forget it.*

I used this technique while writing *Working in Public*, which was a book about the challenges of democracy, wrapped in the allegory of open source software. Back then, at the height of the culture wars, it wasn't socially acceptable to publicly question democracy's virtues, even as it feels trivial to me now, some five years later. One could not ask whether democracy had failed to deliver on its promises – not because malicious actors had coopted the network, or because fascism or misinformation was on the rise, which were socially acceptable ways to critique democracy – but for reasons that had more to do with its fundamental premises.

---

51. Venkatesh Rao, "There Is No Antimemetics Division by qntm," *Ribbonfarm*, May 2, 2024, https://www.ribbonfarm.com/2024/05/02/there-is-no-antimemetics-division-by-qntm/.

Adding more voices to a room, without some additional structure, does not inevitably lead to peace and cooperation, but tribalism and infighting. If we wanted to preserve the democratic values that were essential to the advancement of civilization, we needed to find a different way of expressing them. We needed something different from what had only temporarily *appeared* to work for the first decade or so of the Digital Age, but inevitably fell apart at scale. The end of history had not arrived; our work was not done; the tireless process of solving hard problems for humanity wore on.

These were all the things I wanted to say in *Working in Public*, but could not. So I told the story by using the example of open source software. To be clear: it *is* a book about open source software. But it is also a book about democracy, and while only a smaller group of *Working in Public*'s readers have picked up on this meaning, I am satisfied knowing its message is out there.

SOCIAL PLATFORMS WILL ACT to prevent the spread of ideas that could foster harmful or violent behavior. While these actions are frequently controversial, they are not always driven by political ideology, or even liability concerns. (Having worked in community roles at two social platforms, I can attest firsthand that anyone who thinks they know how to handle content moderation rarely leaves the battlefield unscathed.)

As we saw in Chapter 3, allowing infohazards to fester can enable extreme ideas – like kidnapping and killing a state governor – to evolve in dangerous ways. From an "idea contagion" perspective, wanting to protect networks from harmful infections is a reasonable instinct. Deciding what constitutes "harmful" is the hard part, but that doesn't mean we should denounce the value of moderation itself. It would be like rejecting democracy as a sound form of government, just because we don't like the laws that were made or the politicians that were elected.

Just as the Federal Reserve adjusts interest rates to control inflation or stimulate growth, social platforms adjust their algorithms and moderation policies to manage the flow of information. The goal in both cases is to maintain a delicate balance. Too much openness, and harmful ideas could spread too easily, destabilizing the system – just as runaway inflation can destabilize the economy. Too much control, however, stifles healthy discourse – just as excessively high interest rates can stifle economic growth. And, just as there is no "ideal" interest rate – because rates are dependent upon a constantly evolving, unpredictable system – there is no "ideal" moderation policy. Both require continuous monitoring and adjustments to foster a system that can thrive without tipping into chaos.

Even seemingly innocuous ideas can be dangerous to spread. Ethan Watters' book *Crazy Like Us* posits that certain mental health disorders – like "American-style" depression, post-traumatic stress disorder, and anorexia – are not necessarily intrinsic to individuals, but the result of memetic spread. Watters suggests that these disorders can proliferate when cultural narratives, media depictions, or even well-intentioned medical interventions – like awareness campaigns – normalize or amplify their symptoms. Though it flies against popular wisdom, the implications of Watters' thesis is that it would be better *not* to widely talk about, or even acknowledge, such afflictions, so that we don't infect others.

Some infohazards seem unequivocally bad to share, such as credit card information. Others are somewhat more ambiguous, like the spread of political ideas that could foster violent actions, which must be weighed against our desire to foster a liberal democracy. And still others, like raising awareness of mental health illnesses, are downright counterintuitive.

Just because something is taboo does not mean it is an infohazard, however, and learning to tell the difference is an important skill for each of us – as idea gatekeepers – to sharpen. While it's clear why most people would want to avoid widely disseminating instructions for manufacturing biological weapons, we could have once made a similar argument that the manufacturing of gunpowder should be suppressed, due to its potential to revolutionize warfare and destabilize kingdoms.

How do we know when something is a true infohazard that necessitates suppression, or merely a taboo, which needs time for the network to absorb? As frustrating as it might be, I am not sure there is a clear distinction. Rather, the value of an idea is determined iteratively. How it is classified depends primarily on who is willing to put in the work to socialize it to the general public, and how willing the public is to receive it.

THERE IS SCANT ROOM FOR COMPLEXITY in today's public channels, where being bold and shameless wins you more social points than being thoughtful and nuanced. But nuance doesn't just reside in small, high-context settings where people feel at liberty to say what they really think. Throughout history, societies have relied on the role of "truth-tellers" to bring nuance to large-scale, collective contexts.

A *truth-teller* is an individual to whom we assign the burden of bringing our shared fears, doubts, and taboos to light. Truth-tellers are to antimemes what Girardian scapegoats are to mimetic behavior. In the memetic city, a society that is overwhelmed by mimetic rivalry resolves its tensions by blaming an individual, who serves as a hapless stand-in for their pent-up anger, frustration, and violence. In the antimemetic city, a society that is overwhelmed by *suppression* – unable to express its full range of desires, or acknowledge hard truths that are nonetheless necessary to keep growing and evolving – resolves these tensions through the role of a truth-teller. In both cases, the individual, wittingly or not, is a substitute for the group's desires, rather than representing their own.

Being shameless is not the same as truth-telling. The former is an act of self-interest for personal gain, while the latter is valued for its contribution to the collective interest. The truth-teller says what we are *all* thinking, rather than speaking only for him or herself, or trying to attract attention for shock value. Crucially, truth-tellers also unblock our limiting beliefs and enable us to perceive new, previously antimemetic ideas that can be built and iterated upon. There is a *purpose* to the truths they reveal; they aren't just there to randomly overturn social norms.

Because truth-tellers derive their value from collective interests, their success depends upon the sentiment of the network. They are anchored to a specific place and time. Point out an uncomfortable truth too early, and the truth-teller is swiftly ostracized. Too late, and the truth-teller's role is obsolete.

Like a plant whose roots stretch deep underground, truth-tellers are merely the brightest tip of a long, complex rhizome that the network has likely been nurturing for a long time. In Chapter 2, I described group chats as dense, disparate networks playing a dangerous coordination game. Truth-tellers are most useful at this moment, when the network is ready to flip, but no one group wants to stake their reputation on "calling the hand" in public, because they aren't yet confident about everyone else's position. In this scenario, truth-tellers – unhinged, unpredictable, and therefore oddly trustworthy – can help recalibrate the network. They will happily shout an uncomfortable truth into a crowded room, then twirl off while everyone else hashes it out.

Greta Thunberg played the role of truth-teller when she took the podium at the United Nations' Climate Action Summit in 2019. With her flashing eyes and long hair pulled into a braid, Thunberg uttered her scolding words that reverberated through the internet: "How *dare* you!" She was sixteen years old at the time.

Thunberg was angry that after thirty years of "crystal clear" climate science, our global leaders, despite being embroiled in endless negotiations, had little to show for their efforts. Carbon emission levels had not dropped nearly as quickly as she, nor others, would have liked. "You are failing us," she declared – by which she meant the seasoned, older generations failing the young and future ones – and "we will never forgive you."

Though her speech was received with some bemusement by those who thought it embodied the hysteria of climate activism, Thunberg's words served a very particular, truth-telling purpose. She wasn't trying to scare people; she was there to shame our world leaders for their lack of ambition. In doing so, she created space for people to seriously assess the effectiveness of global climate efforts and emboldened them to search for alternative paths to reaching these goals.

But Thunberg certainly wasn't the first person to lob harsh critiques against the United Nations and their lack of climate progress. Why did her speech stand out where others had not?

The obvious difference – besides the unusual candor and emotion of her speech – is that Thunberg was young, but why does youth make a difference? One could just as easily dismiss perspectives from young people, claiming that they are too inexperienced to be taken seriously, but for some reason, and in certain circumstances, young voices have a particular sway over public opinion, cutting through the noise of hundreds of mature voices who might be thinking or saying the same thing.

Children symbolize purity of intent, and it is this underlying quality that is essential to being recognized as a truth-teller. It was a child, not an adult, who uttered that "The emperor has no clothes!" Despite saying what everyone else already knew, only a child was able to surface this insight, because he was perceived as innocent and honest. Thunberg's activism echoes that of her spiritual predecessor, Severn Cullis-Suzuki, who became known as "The Girl Who Silenced The World For Five Minutes" when, at the age of twelve, she gave a speech about environmentalism to the delegates of the Earth Summit in 1992. Cullis-Suzuki, too, struck a chord in part because her youth made her seem more trustworthy.

A respectful outsider – someone who is perceived as lacking a personal agenda – often carries special gravity. Consider Jane Jacobs, who criticized top-down urban planning approaches in the 1950s, claiming that they were unnatural to how people really lived and operated in cities. Jane Jacobs explicitly lacked formal credentials: she did not have a college degree, and she was often derided by her opponents as a housewife. But it was her lack of credentials that paradoxically made her critiques ring more true. The experts claimed they had studied urban planning and therefore knew what was best for city-dwellers. Jacobs, by contrast, simply used her eyes to look around and describe what she saw, and found that reality was quite different.

While both the urban planners *and* Jacobs could be classified as outsiders, those who push their own agenda – as Jacobs argued the urban planners were doing – often face resistance. They are seen as acting in their own interest, rather than the group's. In order to play the role of truth-teller, an outsider must reflect the community's values.

This purity of intent is not always confined to the childlike or feminine. In Liu Cixin's *The Dark Forest*, humans are trying to find a way to survive an impending invasion from Trisolaris, an alien civilization. Because the Trisolarans can read all human communication, but not private thoughts, the United Nations appoints four individuals to be "Wallfacers," whom they task with each devising a strategy in their minds to defeat the Trisolarans. While three of the Wallfacers have prestigious political and scientific backgrounds, the fourth Wallfacer, Luo Ji, is a lazy, degenerate professor with no obvious accolades. At first, Luo rejects his responsibilities, using his new role selfishly to acquire status and power. But in the end, it is Luo who uncovers an insight that everyone else has overlooked, which leads him to devise the eponymous "dark forest" strategy.

Luo is a sympathetic character in Cixin's book because, compared to his colleagues boasting fancy titles and positions, he seems harmless – even somewhat pathetic. He does not want to be there, and he does not seem especially motivated or curious. Yet somehow, he ends up revealing something interesting about the human condition. Luo's total disconnect from the rest of society is what makes his insights more interesting and credible.

I do not mean to suggest that truth-tellers are necessarily "good" in terms of moral alignment – nor are they even consciously goal-oriented. Lewis Hyde explores one facet of truth-tellers, whom he calls "tricksters," throughout history and mythology in his book, *Trickster Makes This World: Mischief, Myth, and Art*. A trickster dances at the boundaries of our social lives, always there to "cross the line" or "confuse the distinction."[52] There is Prometheus, who stole fire from the gods and gave it to the humans. There is Loki, the Norse god of mischief, who wandered into a banquet of the gods uninvited and demanded their drink. There is Hermes, the Greek god who steals Apollo's cattle on the day he is born and offers the lyre, an instrument he has invented, in exchange – an act that purportedly represents the Greeks' transition from a gift-based to commercial society.

Hyde is careful to distinguish tricksters from the Devil, which he believes are frequently confused for one another. A trickster is not immoral, but *amoral*. His purpose is to remind us of the complexities and ambiguities of life. Although he often causes problems, his liveliness keeps us from getting too stuck in our ways. Tricksters are "the

---

52.   Lewis Hyde, *Trickster Makes This World: Mischief, Myth, and Art* (Farrar, Straus and Giroux, 1998), 7.

creative idiot...the wise fool, the gray-haired baby, the cross-dresser, the speaker of sacred profanities."[53]

Because antimemetic knowledge is so difficult to unearth, it often takes on a sacred quality. In Catholicism, the confessional booth is used to face one's transgressions and doubts – in other words, antimemetic ideas – under the guidance of a priest, who serves as a trusted facilitator. This sacred ritual is called Reconciliation, and it is where antimemes are safely brought to light. In ancient Greece and Rome, oracles and augurs served as intermediaries between the divine and human realms, serving as conduits to speak the difficult truths that could not otherwise be acknowledged by others. In indigenous cultures, shamans serve this intermediary role for their communities by facilitating divine healing and guidance on personal matters.

Throughout human history, societies have instinctively recognized that the most challenging ideas often hold the greatest significance. Rather than being ignored, these ideas take on *especially* high value and importance, precisely because – like precious gems buried deep in the chambers of our psyches – they are so difficult to acquire. Whether they are shrouded in divination practices or coming-of-age ceremonies, antimemes can acquire mystical properties, capable of entering our consciousness only through dedicated spiritual pathways.

If public executions, mobbings, and trials are rituals for the Girardian scapegoat, confessional booths, whistleblowing, and healing ceremonies are rituals for antimemetic truth-tellers. Memes are crass, flashy, and appeal to our reptilian brains. Antimemes are elusive and mysterious, calling out to our souls.

WE STILL HAVE TRUTH-TELLERS TODAY, even in secular contexts. Venture capitalist Katherine Boyle once described the role of the "interesting person," who plays a critical role

---

53. Ibid.

in the "meeting industrial complex." An interesting person – who might be a consultant, academic, or "titled person" (meaning: they've published a book or Substack) – is invited to business meetings to say the things that others in the room aren't able to.[54]

I, and many people I know, have served this role inside organizations. One friend ruefully told me his job was to be a "hood ornament," soothing the nerves of executives and offering candid and witty insights. By the end of my tenure at one company I worked at, my formal job title was simply "Nadia."

I hadn't set out to be, well, "Nadia" as a career, so it was jarring when I first glanced back at my employment history and realized that that was effectively all I'd ever been. At first, I felt that I had failed to make a meaningful impact. But eventually I realized, as Boyle remarked, that the role of an "interesting person" is common within many organizations – you just don't hear about them very often, because no one advertises for them – and that it serves a real purpose. The "interesting person" is a sort of truth-teller whom everyone is inclined to trust, because they have no apparent agenda. They become fast confidantes to executives, middle managers, and entry-level contributors alike. Because they have unusual visibility across the organization, they can observe and express the hidden collective desires that others cannot: the executive because they would be a tyrant, the middle manager because they would risk losing their team, the entry-level contributor because they would endanger their job. While interesting persons may run projects of their own, their true impact is not always measurable through company goals and perfor-

---

54. Katherine Boyle (@ktmboyle), "There's a part of the meeting industrial complex that baffled me when I saw it. There's a genre of consultant, advisor or other adjacent title that exists to be an 'interesting person' to fill up these meetings. Academics, minor elected officials, titled people with books or Substacks," Twitter (now X), August 22, 2024, https://x.com/ktmboyle/status/1826630279919759802.

mance reviews. The real purpose of an interesting person is to shepherd antimemetic knowledge into the light.

When organizations become overly reliant on interesting persons, however, it's a sign that their culture may suffer from a lack of candor or strong leadership – just as any society should not rely too heavily on its priests and soothsayers. Even as Boyle recognizes the value of an interesting person, she worries that, "there aren't a lot of people who can do this. People with original thoughts who have the confidence to say memorable things in these [organizations]. So much so that it's outsourced to people who are retired or tenured or safe in some way. That's the bigger problem."

A lack of truth-tellers, on the other hand, suggests that a community may be overly adapted to the hive mind – as we saw in the case of climate efforts, before Greta Thunberg made her speech at the United Nations. Truth-tellers are an endangered species on our online social platforms, where truth-telling – the art and ritual of grappling openly with complex, nuanced, and difficult ideas – is categorically derided. "Cringe," a term that originated in tandem with the rise of social media, is a uniquely modern concept that refers to doing something that you misjudged as socially acceptable, which then evokes embarrassment from others.

Cringe is more than just internet slang: it's an entirely new, and dangerous, way of operating. Before cringe, people just....tried things, some of which landed, and some which did not. Cringe suppresses the truth-tellers: the chaotic, creative idiots who gleefully prod us to reassess what we think we know and believe. It raises the cost of taking risks and makes it socially expensive to stray outside the boundaries of acceptable behavior.

Cringe reifies the idea that in today's world, we are primarily oriented towards pleasing others and rewarded handsomely for it. That is the role of the shameless shill, and the public web is rife with these characters. Truth-tellers, who often operate outside of conventional norms, are especially vulnerable to being labeled as cringe. This creates a chilling effect, where those with valuable insights hesitate to speak up for fear of ridicule.

Lewis Hyde, writing in 1998, foreshadowed the culture wars when he wrote:[55]

> [T]he erasure of trickster figures, or the unthinking confusion of them with the Devil, only serves to push the ambiguities of life into the background. We may well hope our actions carry no moral ambiguity, but pretending that is the case when it isn't does not lead to greater clarity about right and wrong; it more likely leads to unconscious cruelty masked by inflated righteousness.

The rise of the suburban web, the splitting of ourselves into a thousand cultural narratives – all this gives us only temporary respite from the public web's demands. We may now have quieter corners of the web to experiment and be ourselves, but we still need truth-tellers to help us move the needle at civilizational scale. Societies that celebrate experimentation and tolerate failure are more likely to surface antimemetic ideas, whereas cringe culture narrows the range of acceptable thought. If we hope to do interesting and meaningful things beyond the context of our own tribes, we still need to find room for candor and ambiguity in our public discourse.

Truth-tellers serve a critical role as "interruptors," shaking us out of a dream and forcing us to recalibrate our desires. But without ongoing support from the network, a truth-teller's actions will quickly be forgotten. How do we ensure that surprising new insights remain top-of-mind, for ourselves and for others? That will be our focus in the final chapter.

---

55. Hyde, *Trickster Makes This World: Mischief, Myth, and Art*, 10.

TOWARDS NOT-FORGETTING

6

TWICE A YEAR, we are mysteriously granted or robbed of an hour of sleep: an act that inevitably sparks a burst of outrage, only to be forgotten just as quickly.

Daylight saving time was not, despite popular belief, invented by farmers, who are some of its biggest opponents. Crops must be watered and hay harvested according to the sunlight, not an artificial timekeeping system. Observing daylight saving time, or DST, means losing precious hours to human-dictated schedules instead of following nature's rules.

It's not just farmers who don't like DST. More than two-thirds of Americans would like to abolish the practice of changing our clocks twice a year.[56] Daylight saving time costs the American economy an estimated $434 million per year – one study of miners found that workplace injuries spiked 6 percent after a time shift, leading to 2,600 lost workdays.[57] The American Medical Association recommends eliminating daylight saving time and adopting permanent standard time, citing increased public health and safety risks that include heart attacks and strokes, mood disorders, and motor vehicle crashes.[58]

Despite strong evidence for its repeal, daylight saving time has persisted since the passage of the Uniform Time Act in 1966, which aimed to standardize timekeeping across jurisdictions. Organized attempts to abolish DST have repeatedly failed. In 2022, the United States Senate passed the Sunshine Protection Act with unanimous support, only for it to lapse in the House of Representatives.

---

56. "YouGov Survey: Daylight Savings Time," YouGov, accessed December 21, 2024, https://d3nkl3psvxxpe9.cloudfront.net/documents/tabs_Daylight_Savings_Time_20231027.pdf.
57. David T. Wagner and Christopher M. Barnes, "The Economic Toll of Daylight Saving Time," *The New York Times*, March 6, 2014, https://www.nytimes.com/roo%0Amfordebate/2014/03/06/daylight-saving-time-at-what-cost/the-economic-toll-of-daylight-saving-time.
58. American Medical Association, "AMA calls for permanent standard time," *American Medical Association*, November 15, 2022, https://www.ama-assn.org/press-center/press-releases/ama-calls-permanent-standard-time.

Antimemetics – Why Some Ideas Resist Spreading

Google search interest for "daylight saving time." Momentum builds leading up to the day of the timezone change, only to drop off sharply after.

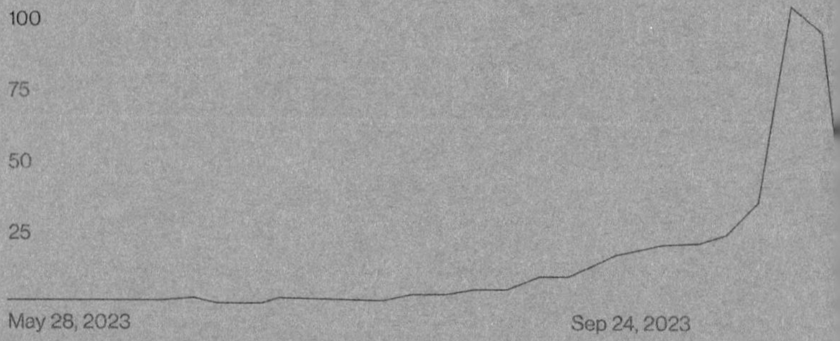

100

75

50

25

May 28, 2023 — Sep 24, 2023

CH.6   Towards Not-Forgetting

Jan 21, 2024   May 19, 2024

At the time of this writing, Congress is valiantly attempting once again to abolish DST with the Sunshine Protection Act of 2023, which faces a similarly uncertain prognosis.

If most people want to get rid of daylight saving time, why can't we pass legislation to fix it? It is a minor annoyance, but a persistent one. Twice a year, the angry tweets and op-eds and thinkpieces come out, decrying the stupidity of the system – only to be forgotten again within days. Nobody can sustain interest, nor retain the problem in their active memory, long enough to make meaningful progress towards abolishing DST.

These "flash floods" of attention can be useful. Antimemes – like our disdain for DST – are hard to notice, so an event that triggers a lot of attention, if only for a short period, creates a rare opportunity to see something we don't usually. When an antimeme becomes a meme, it gives us a limited window to engage with the idea before – like Cinderella's carriage turning back into a pumpkin – it is once again forgotten.

Our inability to abolish DST might seem like a trivial issue, but its absurdity highlights how hard it can be to retain an antimemetic idea, even after truth-tellers have surfaced it into our collective consciousness, and stakeholders are largely aligned. We see this same mechanic play out for more consequential topics, too. After a high-profile mass shooting, interest in gun safety spikes, then is quickly forgotten. Interest in police brutality spikes whenever a relevant news story makes its way into national headlines, but inevitably fizzles. How do we help ourselves remember, and make progress on, the ideas we don't want to forget?

IN QNTM'S *THERE IS NO ANTIMEMETICS DIVISION*, agents who work for the SCP Foundation take "mnestics": drugs that are used to help them remember important ideas that would otherwise slip from their memories. In real life,

we have something like mnestics already: mnemonic devices, from which qntm's fictional drugs take their name:
- *Spaced repetition* is a technique to "flash" an important concept into one's mind by reviewing it intermittently, until it is transferred to long-term memory.
- The *"chain method"* is used to memorize lists by stringing them into a sentence, such as "Please excuse my dear Aunt Sally," or "PEMDAS", which is taught to middle school students to help them remember the order of operations for a mathematical equation (Parentheses, Exponents, Multiplication and Division, Addition and Subtraction).
- *Memory palaces*, or *method of loci*, is a technique frequently used in memory championships, where one visualizes a familiar location, then "places" information throughout the space so that they can recall it later. (I've always been jealous of those who could create memory palaces, as my inability to visualize anything makes this technique seem like a superpower.)

While mnemonic devices are not as deterministic as taking a pill to help us remember, they are strategies we've intentionally developed to help us retain hard-to-remember concepts, even if their histories are mostly forgotten. It is said that the memory palace was invented by the Greek poet Simonides of Ceos around 500 BCE. Simonides attended a banquet; while he stepped outside, the roof fell in, tragically crushing everyone inside. Simonides realized that he could recall who sat where by bringing up the seating arrangement in his visual memory, which made it possible to identify the victims for burial.

    The story of Simonides is likely closer to legend than historical fact, but it marks a real shift where ancient Greeks began to use spatial memory to organize and recall information. It may seem obvious that one could rely on visual imagery to assist in memory recall, but this technique is actually a man-made invention, refined and passed down through centuries of practice.

Mnemonic devices can help us, as individuals, keep slippery ideas at the forefront of our memories. But networks, too, use cultural norms like rituals, traditions, and storytelling to keep themselves from forgetting. How do we collectively decide which ideas are worth remembering?

In the last chapter, we looked at the role of truth-tellers, who direct our attention towards uncomfortable ideas that linger outside our awareness. While truth-tellers are essential to unblock ideas and keep things moving, their lack of agenda is what makes them so trustworthy. Relying solely on the erratic whims of truth-tellers, then, isn't enough to make progress as a civilization. We need proactive strategies for not just remembering, but retaining these ideas.

That is the role of the *champion*, who is the focus of this chapter. Truth-tellers bring new ideas to light, but they often lack the permanence or ambition to formalize them. Champions, on the other hand, ensure that these ideas are preserved and embedded into our institutions. If truth-tellers surface antimemes into our collective consciousness, champions make sure that we keep paying attention to them.

In large, complex systems, not everything can be stored in one place or remembered all at once. If a software database stored all its data in a single place, it would be difficult to access information quickly – like dumping a library's books on the floor, instead of organizing it into sections. Instead, data is split into smaller, distributed parts, or "shards." When the database gets a request, it knows exactly which shard to go to, instead of having to sort through a big, messy pile.

Breaking large swaths of knowledge into smaller parts enables complex systems to scale without being overwhelmed. Just as a database doesn't need each shard to hold all of its data, society doesn't need every individual to keep every important idea top of mind. We each have finite amounts of attention to devote to a limited number of topics, and the "attention market" is both large and liquid, with each person's attention shifting and slipping between topics in intervals as short as seconds. Civilization scales its cultural awareness through "distributed remembering," where we empower champions to curate our attention, which expands our ability to make progress on many different issues at once.

In a highly scaled and distributed marketplace of ideas, which issues we make progress on – the historic moments that come to define our story as a civilization – depends almost entirely on the quality of our champions. *Tell me who your champions are, and I will tell you who you are.*

WE WANT TO BELIEVE THAT networks have some innate morality to them: that the arc of the universe bends inevitably towards justice. While networks are not completely amoral, which specific ideas take hold of a network can often be quite random.

Simler describes the relationship between what's called "spontaneous activation" and transmission rates in his "Going Critical" essay. On its own, spontaneous activation doesn't determine whether an idea takes over a network, which he likens to trying to start a fire in a wet field. If transmission rates are low – i.e. the network isn't receptive to the idea – the idea will die before it spreads. But if the field is very dry (i.e. extremely receptive), one random spark could start a "raging wildfire."[59]

Consider, for example, the book *Seeing Like a State*, written by James C. Scott, which is popular among tech's chattering class of public intellectuals. Scott, a political scientist and anthropologist, published the book as a critique of what he called "high modernism," a mid-20th

---

59.   Simler, "Going Critical."

century movement that emphasizes the use of science and technology to shape society through centralized planning. Scott criticized high modernism for being overly authoritarian and disconnected from what communities actually want, which he felt was better discovered through local knowledge and expertise. His critiques resonated with those in tech, who prefer to reason from first principles and build systems from scratch instead of blindly following the experts.

Scott published *Seeing Like a State* in 1998. But it wasn't until the early 2010s – well over a decade later – that the book suddenly caught on in tech circles. What happened?

The "patient zero" of *Seeing Like a State* was Venkatesh Rao, who published an essay about the book, called "A Big Little Idea Called Legibility," in 2010. Rao focused on Scott's notion of "legibility," or the process of simplifying complex systems, which can make them easier to manage, but also distort them in undesirable ways. "Legibility" caught on as a buzzword in tech, especially among those – like Rao – who took pride in being illegible. *Seeing Like a State* shot to popularity along with it.

One can see how Scott's thesis would resonate with a tech audience. Still, there are likely thousands of as-yet undiscovered books out there that might have caught on for similar reasons. "It's interesting," mused tech writer Jasmine Sun, "how *Seeing Like A State* has made it into the vague tech canon, despite being from a random anarchist anthropologist who specialized in Southeast Asian agrarian societies."[60] How did Rao discover Scott's book in the first place?

Rao explained that in the early 2000s, his wife started, then dropped out of, an anthropology masters program at George Washington University and was

---

60. Noah Putnam, "The Concrete Oasis," *Reboot*, August 18, 2024, https://joinreboot.org/p/the-concrete-oasis.

assigned to read *Seeing Like a State* in her first semester. While she never read the book herself, Rao picked it up from her pile of books and read it a few years later.[61] Rao may have been patient zero, but the popularity of *Seeing Like a State* itself was the product of spontaneous activation.

When I pointed this out on Twitter, a number of commenters rushed to inform me that *Seeing Like a State* had been popular in tech-adjacent libertarian circles and economist blogs, long before Rao wrote his essay. While this is true, none can take direct credit as the "superspreader." *Seeing Like a State*'s dormant popularity in adjacent circles illustrates how a network might be primed for transmission; Rao's wife being assigned a book in her master's program demonstrates how the actual spark that infects a network can be fairly random.

While it may be easier to imagine how tech could become infatuated with a book that validates their values and preferences, let's return to another, even more random example: the rising popularity of the jhanas, the deep meditative states described at the beginning of Chapter 4.

When I first wrote about the jhanas, I was particularly interested in identifying its patient zero, because to casual observers, the practice seemed to have come out of nowhere. I spoke to dozens of people about how they discovered the jhanas. All signs pointed back to one person: an artificial intelligence researcher named Nick Cammarata.

To be clear, there are two overlapping, yet distinct networks that contributed to the recent wave of interest in the jhanas – similarly, perhaps, to the overlapping networks of libertarian economists, and Venkatesh Rao's readership, that together contributed to the popularity of *Seeing Like a*

---

61. Venkatesh Rao (@vgr), "My wife briefly started and dropped out of an anthro masters program at GW ~2003 and this was a first semester text for her. She never read it but I happened to pick it up and read it a year or two later," Twitter (now X), August 19, 2024, https://x.com/vgr/status/1825663123262738737.

State. For the jhanas, one network is the so-called "dharma" community, meaning people who are steeped in traditional meditation lineages. Teachers like Leigh Brasington and Bhante Vimalaramsi helped popularize the jhanas among meditators in recent decades. But they alone do not explain its crossover from meditation circles to a wider audience.

It was Nick Cammarata, an engineer-researcher and meditator with a gentle disposition, who stumbled upon the jhanas in a paper published by the Qualia Research Institute (QRI), a network of researchers interested in consciousness. While he had heard the term before, he hadn't thought much of it until reading the QRI paper, which was about people having extremely different spectrums of pleasure and pain. Curious, he decided to try the jhanas for himself.

After trying and failing for years, Cammarata finally accessed these altered states and was blown away by his experience. He tried searching on Twitter to see who else had commented on them, and was mystified that he couldn't find anything about it. So he started to tweet about the jhanas himself. Though hardly anyone paid attention at first, Cammarata eventually began to amass a following, which led Scott Alexander – whose blog has a large and highly engaged readership – to write about Cammarata's claims. Alexander's post catapulted the jhanas to an even wider (though still tech-adjacent) audience. The sustained buzz caught the attention of a handful of journalists, who were similarly intrigued by the phenomenon. Within a couple of years, the jhanas went from complete obscurity to being featured in mainstream media publications like *The Atlantic*, *Time*, *Vox*, and *Men's Health*.

You may wonder why I have chosen a relatively niche example like the jhanas to highlight the power of champions. The reason is precisely because it is so niche. There is no intrinsic reason why the jhanas should have become popular, relative to other trendy practices in and around tech, like breathwork or Internal Family Systems. Their takeoff can be traced back to the actions of a single meditator who decided to not only take the practice seriously, but to also tell everyone about it.

Even mainstream meditation practices, like mindfulness, owe their prominence to similarly random-seeming events. The reason why you've likely heard of mindfulness, but not the jhanas or any other meditation practice, is because a small group of meditators in the late 1960s and early 1970s – such as Joseph Goldstein and Sharon Salzberg – traveled to India and happened to encounter Vipassana, the tradition from which mindfulness derives, and brought it back to the West. These early influencers went on to found the Insight Meditation Society, where a curious biologist-turned-meditator named Jon Kabat-Zinn studied. Kabat-Zinn adapted their teachings into an eight-week course called Mindfulness-Based Stress Reduction (MBSR), which framed the concept of "mindfulness" in a format that was palatable to a more general audience.

The fact that it is possible for even the most bizarre and improbable ideas to spread through a network should raise our ambitions about what each of us can do as champions. Champions are the firestarters in this story: they help ideas catch on, and, in some cases, create the conditions for unlikely ideas to take off.

A fragmented public narrative doesn't require us to retreat indefinitely into our fortresses. If anything, it is an invitation to engage *more* deeply with the causes we care about most. What seems like scattered noise at first is actually a patchwork of dense networks. Within the context of these smaller networks, it is easier, not harder, to make progress on interesting ideas. We can island-hop the memetic Galapagos; we can scale our capabilities as a network.

FLASH FLOODS OF INTEREST – like the seasonal spikes in interest in daylight saving time – are useful as a short-term mnestic, pushing invisible ideas to the forefront of our minds. But unless they are incorporated into more stable processes, they will dissipate just as they came.

Even the most charged topics – climate change, gun control, the Israel-Palestine conflict – can only sustain themselves on sugary bursts of memetic spread for so long. While these examples are thought of as "hot" political topics, when we consider how they've evolved over longer timelines, it's remarkable how little progress gets made, despite their ability to attract short-term attention. It is not so much that these ideas refuse to spread, but that the fire burns itself out quickly. We are throwing twigs and leaves into the kiln, when what we really need are a few big logs.

When dealing with social issues that span decades, champions will inevitably churn, and this "passing of the baton" can create the illusion of momentum. Like Theseus' ship, there may always be an audience that's eager to engage with these topics, but *who* comprises that audience is constantly changing. Each new wave of champions has a different agenda from their predecessors, and they often prioritize short-term goals over the sustained, coordinated efforts required to achieve lasting change.

College campuses – despite their reputation as memetic hotspots – are perfectly designed to nurture this sort of false progress, where ideas are alive and treading water, but never really evolve or change. This is not a knock on campus culture, but an unfortunate consequence of network design, where the entire college student body turns over every four years. Champions, no matter how passionate and engaged, cannot survive in these settings, because just as they get their bearings, they are ejected from the network.

The short-term memory of college campuses works in favor of administrators on internal issues like tuition costs, management of the endowment, or campus conduct. But even external political issues assume a certain zombie-like quality on college campuses. There will always be a climate club, a human rights club, a Hillel club – but these function more like dollhouses in which to play champion. No memetic fire can sustain itself solely among college students – even when they spread to other campuses – because, as students graduate, they inevitably run out of kindling.

Parenting is another example of an antimemetic ecosystem. Parents are a notoriously engaged demographic overall, but the members of each child's age group are constantly rotating. This makes them a fickle constituency, especially when it comes to policies that are age-specific, such as those related to pregnancy and new parents – a relatively short phase in a parent's life.

Maternity leave, for example, has been shown to substantially decrease infant mortality rates, particularly for the children of college-educated and married mothers.[62] Three-quarters of Americans support federal paid leave for new parents, and there is bipartisan support in Congress for such a program. Despite widespread support for the idea overall, the United States has yet to enact a federal paid leave policy, in large part because legislators cannot agree on the specific form it should take.[63] Though the reasons behind this lack of consensus are complex, it does not help that the constituency of voters who care most about it – expecting parents, and those with children under one year old – is transient, just like college students. Without sustained attention from a broader base of supporters, these issues become calcified as perpetually "hot topics" in the political discourse, against which we can never seem to make progress.

But not all ephemeral networks are doomed to this state. Elected government officials in the United States, like

---

62. Maya Rossin, "The Effects of Maternity Leave on Children's Birth and Infant Health Outcomes in the United States," *Journal of Health Economics* 30, no. 2 (2011): 221-239, https://doi.org/10.1016/j.jhealeco.2011.01.005.
63. "Cato Institute 2018 Paid Leave Survey," Cato Institute, accessed December 20, 2024, https://www.cato.org/sites/cato.org/files/survey-reports/pdf/cato2018paidleavesurvey-updated.pdf.

college students or parents, often cycle out every few years. Yet while the political machine is slow, it nevertheless turns, because institutional memory resides among their staff, who float through the halls of the Capitol and build careers that can outlast any one politician's. It is often said that a politician's staff is where all the real progress is made, because they stick around long enough to understand how things really work and advocate relentlessly on behalf of the issues they care about most.

The successful passage of the Affordable Care Act (ACA) in 2010, for example, was significantly influenced by long-serving staffers who had been working on healthcare reform for years, well before Barack Obama's presidency. Two of the most prominent architects of the ACA were Senator Max Baucus, who chaired the Finance Committee, and Senator Ted Kennedy, a lifelong advocate of healthcare reform. Baucus and Kennedy started collaborating early on, meeting at Kennedy's Washington home to outline their strategy. But also in attendance that day was Elizabeth Fowler, chief health counsel to Baucus, who had spent her entire career working in healthcare, domestically and abroad. She was intimately familiar with how other countries' systems were designed, and she had worked with several other senators before Baucus.[64] Fowler had already worked with Kennedy on a Medicare drug bill many years before, and their familiarity with each other helped build trust between parties. Kennedy, too, relied on staffers such as Michael Myers, who worked in his office for more than two decades, to bring his vision to life after Kennedy passed away in 2009 from brain cancer, just before the bill's passage.[65] The knowledge and relationships that

---

64. Dov Weinryb Grohsgal, "Interview with Elizabeth Fowler," Obama Presidency Oral History, Columbia University in the City of New York, 2020, https://obamaoralhistory.columbia.edu/interviews/elizabeth-fowler.
65. "Interviews: Michael Myers and Stuart Altman," *Frontline*, PBS, April 13, 2010, https://www.pbs.org/wgbh/pages/frontline/obamasdeal/interviews/myers-altman.html.

Baucus and Kennedy's staff developed across multiple administrations helped them accomplish one of the most complex and far-reaching healthcare reforms in United States history.

Institutional design influences what we remember or forget. News feeds, for example, are designed for forgetting. They are optimized for breadth of exposure, rather than depth of engagement. Although social posts can go viral in the moment, once we scroll past them, they can be hard to find again – which means there is plenty of information that's technically publicly available online, but difficult to recover because it is not well-indexed.

Conversely, photo apps like Apple's Photos or Google Photos – which could have easily become a black box of memories – are designed to resurface photos from our past. There is nothing innately ephemeral about social posts, any more than the countless photos we've taken are innately memorable. The difference is in the design of our systems, which have downstream effects on how we engage with the ideas contained within.

In Chapter 3, we learned about inverted containment in the TINAD universe, where isolation chambers offer a safe haven from the destructive influence of antimemes roaming about in the world. But these chambers aren't just empty, sterile rooms. They're filled with artifacts: paperwork, Post-Its, diagrams scribbled on the wall with marker pens. There are notes left behind by prior visitors, chronicling everything they know before their memories are wiped and the forgetting begins again. These artifacts are a gift to their future selves, and to anyone else who might come across the same problem and try to solve it. Even if one person disappears, our collective memory carries on.

PROTOCOLS GIVE US A STRUCTURED WAY to manage large amounts of information that we want to remember, which frees our attention to focus on other things.[66] Like mnemonic devices, although protocols seem like an intuitive feature of society today, they, too, had to be invented.

Protocolization boomed with the onset of industrialization, or what historian James Beniger called the "control revolution": a need to gain control over the sudden explosion of information created by new manufacturing processes. Standardized forms and TCP/IP, for example, are protocols for collecting and handling data. Management theory and organizational governance – whether hierarchy or holocracy – are protocols for coordinating people. Laws are protocols that tell us what the consequences are for various actions that a citizen might take.

Protocols save us time and attention, but they require enormous trust in the quality of the system itself. Over time, if protocols are not continuously revisited and revised, they can become crufty and dated. But protocols can be difficult to modify, even when they've clearly drifted from their original purpose, because the longer we use them, the more accustomed we are to the easy, mindless way of doing things. We may even find ways to retroactively justify their legitimacy in order to keep things the way they are.

Recycling protocols, for example, were initially promoted as a way to reduce landfill waste and conserve resources. Over time, they became not just an environmental policy, but a moral imperative for many people. Sorting paper from plastic and rinsing out containers, even in situations where recycling is demonstrated to be ineffective, became acts of virtue signaling: a way to demonstrate one's commitment to protecting the environment. Instead of evaluating whether recycling actually works in every con-

---

66. This section on protocols was originally explored in the essay "Dangerous Protocols," which I wrote and published as part of the Ethereum Foundation's *Summer of Protocols* 2023 research program – Nadia Asparouhova, "Dangerous Protocols," Summer of Protocols, 2023, https://summerofprotocols.com/dangerous-protocols-web.

text, people became preoccupied with whether they, and others, were "doing the right thing."

The derisive term for the Byzantine systems that protect these behaviors is *bureaucracy*: a complex system of protocols that no one person understands, which means it cannot be easily dismantled. Bureaucracies are antimemetic systems. Their purpose is to automate decision making, which they accomplish so well that even when we *want* to change the system, it can be near-impossible to wrap our minds around its complexity. Complaints, no matter how serious in the moment, are filed and forgotten.

Rather than a memeplex – Dawkins' term for a group of memes that replicate together and reinforce each other – bureaucracies can be thought of as a type of *antimemeplex*, in which a series of antimemes act together to stay hidden from our awareness. If a supermeme is like a black hole that demands our attention over all else, an antimemeplex completely repels our attention at an impressive scale. Explicit resistance to bureaucracy tends to be ineffective, because there is no clear authority to overthrow. Because nobody is singularly responsible for bad protocols, participants can get trapped indefinitely in suboptimal outcomes.

Writer and artificial intelligence researcher Eliezer Yudkowsky called these "inadequate equilibria" in his book of the same name – "a sticky, stable equilibrium of *everyone* acting insane in a way that's secretly a sane response to everyone else acting insane" – where civilizations get stuck at a local maximum.[67] Yudkowsky directs his ire towards the United States medical system, which he calls "the most broken system that still works ever recorded in human history," and academic science, which is stuck in "a Nash equilibrium that it wandered into, which includes statistical methods that were invented in the first half of the 20th century and editors not demanding that people cite replica-

---

67.   Eliezer Yudkowsky, *Inadequate Equilibria: Where and How Civilizations Get Stuck* (Machine Intelligence Research Institute, 2017), 54.

tions."[68, 69] No single entity *caused* these protocols to end up where they are today, but no one participant can defy it, except at personal cost. Scott Alexander called these "Moloch" problems, named after an Allen Ginsberg poem, in which "Every single citizen hates the system, but for lack of a good coordination mechanism it endures."[70]

We can say, over and over again, that our healthcare system is a nightmare, Transportation Security Administration (TSA) rules are outdated, or that academic journal publishing is broken, but these systems are unlikely to change without the help of champions, who – like the congressional staffers who helped architect the ACA – know the system well enough to tame it. It is why figures like Robert Moses, who dare to take on these entrenched systems, transfix our imagination. Moses, who is widely considered the mastermind behind the building of New York City in the mid-1900s, understood how to navigate bureaucracies with incredible precision. He knew not only how these systems worked, but how to bend them to his will. Despite never holding elected office, Moses reshaped New York City's infrastructure through his deep understanding of the processes driving its policy, funding, and public works. He knew how to leverage obscure rules, exploit loopholes, and attract resources in ways that made him extremely powerful.

Though his legacy is controversial, Moses demonstrates how champions can drive the overhaul of complex systems: by patiently working within and around the structures in ways that most people don't have the stamina for, or don't even notice exist. Moses wasn't superhuman; he just paid attention to the things that others did not. He was able to grapple with the kind of intricacy that overwhelms most people, which is why true reform in systems like

68. Ibid., 45.
69. Ibid., 63.
70. Scott Alexander, "Meditations on Moloch," *Slate Star Codex*, July 30, 2014, https://slatestarcodex.com/2014/07/30/meditations-on-moloch/.

healthcare, academia or politics often depends on inside players who aren't distracted by surface-level noise.

From the outside, bureaucracies look like unintelligible noise. They are mystifying, alien machines whose convoluted structures deter us from examining their inner workings. Untangling these processes is not for the faint of heart. Most problems, to most people, seem like more trouble than they're worth.

But to the right champion, even the most labyrinthine system feels like an invitation to create something extraordinary. Everyone has at least one system for which this is true, which means that all of us have the potential to champion an antimemetic idea more deeply. You will know it when looking at the problem makes your heart expand with possibilities, rather than shrink away – when, instead of feeling overwhelmed, you feel a spark of curiosity.

The world, after all, is more than just what we inherit. It's what we choose to notice, nurture, and build. Everything around us – for worse, yes, but also for the better – is made up of where we direct our attention. If we learn to channel it wisely, we can decide what type of future we want to see.

Antimemetics – Why Some Ideas Resist Spreading

Acknowledgements

I told almost no one about this book, which makes this section quite small. Thanks to Yancey Strickler and the Dark Forest Collective for giving this book a home, without which it never would have escaped my desktop folder. Thanks to Evan Miyazono, Applied Divinity Studies, Uri Bram, Andy Matuschak, and Sebastian Bensusan. Thanks to Kevin Simler for writing the first great nonfiction book about antimemetics, and to qntm – who has no relationship to this book, but whose work I admire – for being the node that spontaneously infected a network.

Antimemetics – Why Some Ideas Resist Spreading

Introduction: Escaping Containment

- Appleton, Maggie. "Cozy Web." *Maggie Appleton*, accessed December 20, 2024. https://maggieappleton.com/cozy-web.
- Armstrong-Novak, JoDee, Hui Yu Juan, Kaila Cooper, and Pamela Bailey. "Healthcare Personnel Hand Hygiene Compliance: Are We There Yet?" *Current Infectious Disease Reports* vol. 25 (2023): 123-129. https://doi.org/10.1007/s11908-023-00806-8.
- Halilovic, Ajdina. "People Who Can't Picture Sound in Their Minds." *Nautilus*, February 20, 2024. https://nautil.us/people-who-cant-picture-sound-in-their-minds-517529/.
- Rao, Venkatesh. "The Extended Internet Universe." *Contraptions*, May 24, 2019. https://contraptions.venkateshrao.com/p/the-extended-internet-universe.
- SCP Database Wiki. "Antimemetics." Accessed December 20, 2024. https://scp-db.fandom.com/wiki/Antimemetics.
- SCP Foundation Wiki. "SCP-055." Accessed December 20, 2024. https://scp-wiki.wikidot.com/scp-055.
- S. S. Walrus. "From the Files of Site 19." Archived on *archive.is*. Accessed December 20, 2024. https://archive.is/QD9UF.
- Strickler, Yancey. "The Dark Forest Theory of the Internet." *Medium*, May 20, 2019. https://ystrickler.medium.com/the-dark-forest-theory-of-the-internet-7dc3e68a7cb1.

Chapter 1: Hidden City

- Barnes, Connor, and Peter Limberg. "Memetic Tribes and Culture War 2.0." *Medium*, September 13, 2018. https://medium.com/s/world-wide-wtf/memetic-tribes-and-culture-war-2-0-14705c43f6bb.
- Bowman, Brooke and Alex Grin. "Vibecamp: Looking Forward w/ Brooke Bowman & Alex Grin." Moderated by Peter Limberg. Posted June 22, 2022, by The Stoa. YouTube. https://www.youtube.com/watch?v=cuaR-BuESOx0.
- Cowen, Tyler. "The changes in vibes — why did they happen?" *Marginal Revolution*, July 17, 2024. https://marginalrevolution.com/marginalrevolution/2024/07/the-changes-in-vibes-why-did-they-happen.html.
- Federal Emergency Management Agency (FEMA). *Natural Hazard Mitigation Saves: An Independent Study to Assess the Future Savings from Mitigation Activities*. Accessed December 20, 2024. https://www.fema.gov/sites/default/files/2020-07/mitigation-saves_poster16x20_180611.pdf.
- Gioia, Ted. "Why Do I Keep Saying the Culture is Stagnating?" *The Honest Broker*, August 30, 2023. https://www.honest-broker.com/p/why-do-i-keep-saying-the-culture.
- Haigney, Sophie. "How Group Chats Rule the World." *The New York Times Magazine*, January 16, 2024. https://www.nytimes.com/2024/01/16/magazine/group-chats.html.
- Hardy, Rob. "Memes We Live By." *Vibecamp*. Accessed December 20, 2024, https://vibe.camp/.
- Krishnan, Rohit. "Seeing Like a Network." *Strange Loop Canon*, June 19, 2024. https://www.strangeloopcanon.com/p/seeing-like-a-network.
- Krishnan, Sriram. "Group chats rule the world." *Sriram Krishnan*, May 19, 2024. https://sriramk.com/

- group-chats-rule-the-world.
- Limberg, Peter. "Meme to Vibe: A Philosophical Report." *Less Foolish*, March 6, 2023. https://lessfoolish.substack.com/p/meme-to-vibe-a-philosophical-report.
- Park, Se Jung, Yon Soo Lim, Han Woo Park. "Comparing Twitter and YouTube networks in information diffusion: The case of the 'Occupy Wall Street' movement." *Technological Forecasting and Social Change* vol. 95 (2019): 208-217. https://doi.org/10.1016/j.techfore.2015.02.003.
- Silverstein, Ken. "Off Leash: Inside the Secret, Global, Far-Right Group Chat." *The New Republic*, May 30, 2024. https://newrepublic.com/article/182008/erik-prince-secret-global-group-chat-off-leash.
- Sung, Hannah. "The Last Place Left Online for Real Conversation." *The New York Times*, August 13, 2022. https://www.nytimes.com/2022/08/13/opinion/group-chats-social-media.html.

Chapter 2: Drag Coefficient

- Forte, Tiago (@fortelabs). "The key to Twitter is joining an informal cabal of mutually retweeting people with aligned agendas. Then you all interact with each other as a kind of performance art. But you can't ask or apply formally. It's all implicit, like collusion around price fixing." Twitter (now X), June 13, 2019. https://x.com/fortelabs/status/1139234130682699777.
- Moldbug, Mencius. "A formalist manifesto." *Unqualified Reservations*, April 24, 2007. https://www.unqualified-reservations.org/2007/04/formalist-manifesto-originally-posted/.
- Qntm. *There Is No Antimemetics Division*. Self-published, 2021.
- Simler, Kevin. "Going Critical." *Melting Asphalt*, May 13, 2019. https://meltingasphalt.com/interactive/going-critical/.

Chapter 3: Memetic Galapagos

- Yale Program on Climate Change Communication. "Global Warming's Six Americas." Accessed December 20, 2024. https://climatecommunication.yale.edu/about/projects/global-warmings-six-americas/.

Chapter 4: We Are Our Attention

- Burnett, D. Graham, Alyssa Loh, and Peter Schmidt. "Powerful Forces Are Fracking Our Attention. We Can Fight Back." *The New York Times*, November 24, 2023. https://www.nytimes.com/2023/11/24/opinion/attention-economy-education.html.
- Emmons, Robert A. and Michael E. McCullough. "Counting Blessings Versus Burdens: An Experimental Investigation of Gratitude and Subjective Well-Being in Daily Life." *Journal of Personality and Social Psychology* 84, no. 2 (2003): 377-389. https://greatergood.berkeley.edu/pdfs/GratitudePDFs/6Emmons-BlessingsBurdens.pdf.
- Friends of Attention. "About the Friends of Attention." Accessed December 20, 2024. https://www.friendsofattention.net/about.
- Hanson, Robin and Kevin Simler. *The Elephant in the Brain: Hidden Motives in Everyday Life*. Oxford University Press, 2018.
- Hart Research Associates and Public Opinion Strategies. "Americans' Knowledge Of And Attitudes

- Toward Antibiotic Resistance: A report of findings from a national survey and two focus groups." The Pew Health Group, November 2012. https://www.pewtrusts.org/-/media/legacy/uploadedfiles/phg/content_level_pages/in_the_news/abxpollsummarypdf.pdf.
- Jarow, Oshan. "What if you could have a panic attack, but for joy?" *Vox*, June 7, 2024. https://www.vox.com/future-perfect/354069/what-if-you-could-have-a-panic-attack-but-for-joy.
- Lambe, Kathryn Ann, Sinéad Lydon, Caoimhe Madden, et al. "Hand Hygiene Compliance in the ICU: A Systematic Review." *Critical Care Medicine* 47, no. 9 (2019): 1251-1257. https://doi.org/10.1097/CCM.0000000000003868.
- Odell, Jenny. *How to Do Nothing: Resisting the Attention Economy.* Melville House, 2020

Chapter 5: Sacred Knowledge

- Bostrom, Nick. "Information Hazards: A Typology of Potential Harms from Knowledge." *Review of Contemporary Philosophy*, vol. 10 (2011): 44-79. https://nickbostrom.com/information-hazards.pdf.
- Boyle, Katherine (@ktmboyle). "There's a part of the meeting industrial complex that baffled me when I saw it. There's a genre of consultant, advisor or other adjacent title that exists to be an 'interesting person' to fill up these meetings. Academics, minor elected officials, titled people with books or Substacks." Twitter (now X), August 22, 2024. https://x.com/ktmboyle/status/1826630279919759802.
- Burja, Samo. "Intellectual Dark Matter." *Samo Burja*, July 16, 2019. https://samoburja.com/intellectual-dark-matter/.
- Hyde, Lewis. *Trickster Makes This World: Mischief, Myth, and Art.* Farrar, Straus and Giroux, 1998.
- Pardes, Arielle. "The Debacle Sums Up Tech's Race Issues." *Wired*, June 29, 2020. https://www.wired.com/story/eye-mouth-eye/.
- Rao, Venkatesh. "There Is No Antimemetics Division by qntm." *Ribbonfarm*, May 2, 2024. https://www.ribbonfarm.com/2024/05/02/there-is-no-antimemetics-division-by-qntm/.

Chapter 6: Towards Not-Forgetting

- Alexander, Scott. "Meditations on Moloch." *Slate Star Codex*, July 30, 2014. https://slatestarcodex.com/2014/07/30/meditations-on-moloch/.
- American Medical Association. "AMA calls for permanent standard time." *American Medical Association*, November 15, 2022. https://www.ama-assn.org/press-center/press-releases/ama-calls-permanent-standard-time.
- Asparouhova, Nadia. "Dangerous Protocols." *Summer of Protocols*, 2023. https://summerofprotocols.com/dangerous-protocols-web.
- Cato Institute. "Cato Institute 2018 Paid Leave Survey." Accessed December 20, 2024. https://www.cato.org/sites/cato.org/files/survey-reports/pdf/cato2018paidleavesurvey-updated.pdf.
- PBS. "Interviews: Michael Myers and Stuart Altman." *Frontline*, April 13, 2010. https://www.pbs.org/wgbh/pages/frontline/obamasdeal/interviews/myers-altman.html.
- Putnam, Noah. "The Concrete Oasis." *Reboot*, August 18, 2024.

https://joinreboot.org/p/the-concrete-oasis.

- Rao, Venkatesh (@vgr). "My wife briefly started and dropped out of an anthro masters program at GW ~2003 and this was a first semester text for her. She never read it but I happened to pick it up and read it a year or two later." Twitter (now X), August 19, 2024. https://x.com/vgr/status/1825663123262738737.
- Rossin, Maya. "The Effects of Maternity Leave on Children's Birth and Infant Health Outcomes in the United States." *Journal of Health Economics* 30, no. 2 (2011): 221-239. https://doi.org/10.1016/j.jhealeco.2011.01.005.
- Wagner, David T. and Christopher M. Barnes. "The Economic Toll of Daylight Saving Time." *The New York Times*, March 6, 2014. https://www.nytimes.com/roo%0Amfordebate/2014/03/06/daylight-saving-time-at-what-cost/the-economic-toll-of-daylight-saving-time.
- Weinryb Grohsgal, Dov. "Interview with Elizabeth Fowler." Obama Presidency Oral History, Columbia University in the City of New York, 2020. https://obamaoralhistory.columbia.edu/interviews/elizabeth-fowler.
- YouGov. "YouGov Survey: Daylight Savings Time." Accessed December 21, 2024. https://d3nkl3psvxxpe9.cloudfront.net/documents/tabs_Daylight_Savings_Time_20231027.pdf.
- Yudkowsky, Eliezer. *Inadequate Equilibria: Where and How Civilizations Get Stuck*. Machine Intelligence Research Institute, 2017.

Antimemetics – Why Some Ideas Resist Spreading

Editor	Yancey Strickler
Designer	Leïth Benkhedda
Publisher	The Dark Forest Collective
Printer	Die Keure by INNIgroup
Year	2025 – Second Printing
ISBN	979-8-9929364-0-7